FASHION OUTLINES

DRESS CUTTING

by

THE BLOCK PATTERN SYSTEM

by
Margaret C. Ralston

edited by
Jules & Kaethe Kliot

**A system of scientific dressmaking
explored through the classical styles of
the late 1920's and early 1930's**

LACIS
PUBLICATIONS

3163 Adeline Street, Berkeley, CA 94703
© 1990   Jules Kliot

ISBN   0-916896-32-3

INTRODUCTION

A new era in women's fashions was to find its beginnings after the great war of 1918. With no uncertainty, the mechanical devices designed to create the "ideal" female form were cast away and the peculiar innocence of a new beginning was to take hold in a basic "no form" model, where style would be determined by the geometric line which was to dominate, filling its own complimentary nitch in the "Art Deco" movement.

The new ideal 'barrel' line, emphasized the boyish look with 'flatteners' replacing the previous devices to reinforce this new mode. The waist disappeared, and if the body was divided at all, it would be at the hips. The long skirt lengths of the teens would be discarded by the mid twenties as the scandalous short skirts demanded a renewed acknowledgement that this new women had to be reckoned with. Along with the boyish figure, came the close cut hair, and the snug fitting hat. The emphasis was on line and geometry, which was carried through to facial make up, where the pencilled eyebrow became so characteristic.

The radical style changes forced the closing of the established Paris couture houses of the "belle epoque", with names such as Doucet, Poiret and Delayed, succumbing to the new trends.

The new styles found their new mentors in such names as 'Coco" Chanel and Elsa Schiaparelli who became the driving force behind the new woman, the woman who was no longer the show piece of the male but now an integral part of the social conscience. This was no stronger realized then in the migration of fashion into the 'working-class' vocabulary. The simplicity of style related to simplicity of creating with the popular acceptance of home sewing as it related to fashion.

By the end of the twenties, what demanded to be heard was heard, and the stylized outlines could accept relaxation without surrender. The hemline dropped, the waist was allowed to be recognized and softness in line and edge could be tolerated. Even the hair was allowed to grow again as female was allowed to be differentiated from male. This period seemed to encompass the best of all worlds, with the attributes of style, comfort, femininity and 'socially aware being' all working together.

This period would be followed by the years of world-wide doubt and uncertainly as the human focus would be on unemployment, depression, and the rise of tyranny with fashion taking a back seat for a whole generation.

This book explores the 'block pattern' method in developing the flat pattern for garment fabrication. It uses the classic styles of the late twenties and eary thirties in describing this technique with the basic patterns presented in a conceptual manner.

The method is as relevant today as it was sixty years ago as are the fashion concepts. This book should be a valuable resources to both sewing enthusiasts who simply wish to recreate the wearables illustrated, as well as costume designers who will find the method refreshing and the patterns a starting point for creating their own innovative fashions.

This book, without the fashion plates, was originally published as:

DRESS CUTTING by Margaret C. Ralston, Lecturer in dressmaking and needlework, National Society's training College for Teachers of Domestic Subjects, Hampstead, London, published in 1932 by Sir Isaac Pitman & Sons, Ltd. This work is included complete with fashion plate supplements from contemporary magazines.

Reference to illustrations is as follows:

Cover   Delineator, January 1927
Page ii   Delineator, May 1927
Page iv   Lower Right: McCalls, July 1927
     Upper Left: McCalls, September 1928
Page vi   Center: Delineator, December 1928
     Perimeter: Ladies Home Journal, January 1929
Page viii   Upper Left: Needlecraft, May 1930
     Left Center: Needlecraft, July 1930
     Lower Right: Needlecraft, May 1930
     Lower Left: Delineator, November 1929
Page 72   Butterick, 1931

Jules & Kaethe Kliot

iv

PREFACE

Most women have, at some time in their lives, attempted to make their own dresses, and many have continued to do so with success. Some, however, have given up the attempt because they could not find a pattern to suit them, and did not know how to make one.

The expression "Scientific Dressmaking" seems to strike terror to the amateur dressmaker's soul, but it is hoped that the method of pattern-cutting explained in this book will be sufficiently straightforward and simple to appeal to the most nervous home dressmaker. What is more, it is hoped that the patterns produced will prove to fit so well that another bug-bear of the amateur, fitting, will be practically removed.

This method has been arrived at after many years of teaching young women the art of dressmaking. It was found that though they had plenty of good ideas and were only too keen to carry them out, they refused to sustain any interest in pattern-making unless they could quickly visualize the pattern as a potential garment for themselves.

One foundation draft is necessary, but a simple jumper pattern presents no difficulties and is quickly produced.

The method of converting a straight strip of paper into the pattern of a flared skirt makes a fascinating lesson, and very soon the possibility of the flat pattern adaptation is grasped and proves of lasting interest.

To illustrate the method it has been necessary to use the styles of the moment. As far as possible these have been chosen from types which, in some form or another, are always with us. It is hoped that, when the designs shown are out of date, it will still be possible, by working on similar lines, to get an up-to-date style which will give satisfaction.

I should like to dedicate this book to the many bright young things who have passed through my classes, and who have always been so ready to experiment on any style, no matter how intricate.

M. C. R.

CONTENTS

CHAP.   PAGE

I. PATTERN MAKING I

II. MEASUREMENTS 2

III. BLOCK PATTERN 7
    1. Jumper.
    2. Sleeve.

IV. SKIRT CUTTING 11
    1. Flared skirt.
    2. Costume skirt.
    3. Flared skirt with hip yoke.
    4. Costume skirt with hip yoke.

V. ADAPTATION OF BLOCK PATTERN 18

VI. BLOUSES 20
    1. Simple blouse.
    2. Blouse with shoulder straps and front fulness.

VII. DRESSES 24
    1. Coat overall.
    2. Dress with skirt flared from waist line.
    3. Dress with skirt flared from hip line.
    4. Dress with hip yoke and flared skirt.
    5. Dress with godet skirt.
    6. Dress with hip yoke, panels at back and front and circular side pieces.
    7. Dress with flounces.
    8. Dress with flared skirt 54 in. wide at hem.

VIII. SLEEVES 51
    1. Fitted sleeve with dart.
    2. Fitted sleeve with gathers at elbow.

IX. COLLARS AND CAPES 53
    1. Detachable polo collar.
    2. Rever collar.
    3. Roll collar with points.
    4 and 5. Simple round collars with pointed fronts.
    6 and 7. Bertha collars.
    8. Cape with shoulder dart.

X. PLEATED SKIRTS 60
    1. Yoked skirt with front pleats.
    2. Four-gored skirt with inserted pleats at seams.

XI. GODETS 68
    1. Simple godets.
    2. Godets with shaped top.

DRESS CUTTING

CHAPTER I

PATTERN MAKING

THE expert dress designer obtains her best results by draping and cutting the material on the model; but this requires a skill and experience which is beyond the scope of the average home dressmaker.

Drafting also presents many complications to the amateur, but she will not find the draft of the simple jumper pattern in any way difficult, and with it as foundation or block pattern she may evolve almost any other pattern she may choose.

Just as the expert builds up her design on the model so must the home dressmaker build up her pattern on the block pattern.

The block pattern must be regarded by her as a flat representation of the figure, and the cutter should be so familiar with it that she can visualize on it the design which she wishes to carry out.

It is probably unnecessary to say that the amateur dressmaker must have an ever-receptive mind, ready to grasp new ideas and, if necessary, to alter practically all her preconceived notions of what is right and wrong in dress cutting.

It is said that fashions always work in cycles and nothing is ever new, but there is always something different about the latest fashion, and it is that that makes the subject of such absorbing interest to most women.

CHAPTER II

MEASUREMENTS

No patterns can be reliable and, therefore, no dress can give satisfaction if the measurements are not correctly taken. A definite list of measurements is taken for the jumper block pattern, and for the sleeve and skirt.

For the adaptation of these the cutter must study her style very closely, and decide for herself on the extra measurements which will be necessary to make an accurate pattern.

Measurements for Jumper Block Pattern.

A tape must always be pinned round the natural waist line before taking the measurement. The *lower* edge of the tape defines the waist line.

If desired, another tape may be pinned round the figure at a level of 7 in. below the waist line to define the hip line.

The measurements given below are numbered according to the numbers shown in the diagram. (Fig. 1, *a* and *b*.) The essential measurements and the method of taking them are as follows—

No.	Measurement	Method of Taking	Average Size
			in.
1	Nape to waist . .	Taken from the bone at the base of the back of neck to the waist line	15½
2	Nape to hip . .	Add 7 in. to above measurement . .	22½
3	Width of bust . .	Pass the tape round the fullest part of the figure, keeping it well up under the arm-pit. Take this quite loosely	36
4	Width of back . .	Mark a point midway between shoulder and under-arm point. At this level measure across the back from the points where the sleeve should be set in	12
5	Width of chest . .	Taken across the front at the same level as the width of back was taken. Measure from the muscle in front of the arm	14
6	Width of hip . .	Taken quite loosely 7 in. below the waist line	40
7	Shoulder length .	Taken from the neck line along the shoulder to the point where the sleeve is inset. This is not essential but an aid to an accurate draft	5

Taking Measurements.

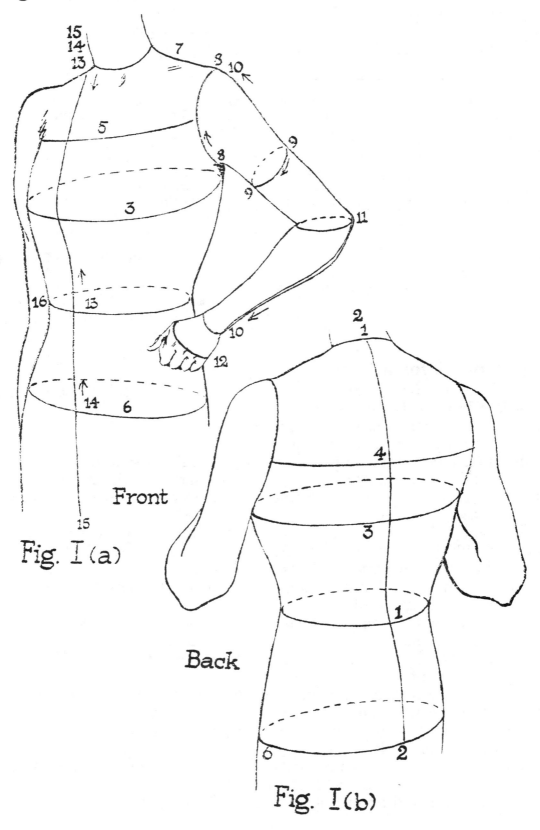

Front

Fig. I (a)

Back

Fig. I (b)

Sleeve Measurements.

No.	Measurement	Method of Taking	Average Size
			in.
8	Armhole . . .	Taken round the top of the arm rather tightly, and keeping the tape well up over the shoulder bone	16
9	Width of sleeve .	Bend the arm so that the upper muscle is fully developed. Take the measurement round the widest part and add 3 in., as an easy measurement is essential	15
10	Length of sleeve .	Taken from the top of the arm at a point about 1 in. behind the shoulder seam. Carry the tape down the back of the bent arm to the wrist	25
11	Elbow . . .	(For tight sleeves only.) Bend the elbow and measure tightly round the widest part	12
12	Wrist . . .	(For tight sleeves only.) Measure round the knuckles of the closed hand. This should be the smallest possible measurement to allow the sleeve to slip over the wrist	8

Measurements for a Dress.

It is assumed that the cutter has already made a block pattern which she intends to adapt for the dress.

She will need some extra measurements, but these will vary according to the particular style of dress chosen.

It is usually necessary to pin a tape round the waist and hip, but it must be clearly understood that these are not necessarily at the natural waist and hip line but at the level which seems correct according to the style which is being produced.

These tapes are of the greatest importance, and the person who is to wear the dress should be consulted as to their position, as the entire line of the dress will be spoilt if the waist and hip lines are not only at the level which follows the fashion of the moment, but also at a level which is becoming to the particular figure which is being fitted.

It cannot be too strongly emphasized that the greatest care must be taken in measuring both waist and hip, but more particularly the hip. This must be taken loosely enough to give freedom of movement, as no extra width is allowed in the adaptation as a rule.

The length measurements taken for the adaptations are always taken in front from the highest point of the shoulder. It is seldom necessary to take the back length as well if the method of adaptation is followed according to the instructions in this book.

The following extra measurements are usually needed when adapting the block pattern to make a dress pattern.

They are numbered according to the numbered points in Fig. 1 (a).

No.	Measurement	Method of Taking	Average Size
			in.
13	Shoulder to waist.	From the highest point of the front shoulder to the waist line	—
14	Shoulder to hip	Continue the above measure to the hip line	—
15	Shoulder to hem	Continue the above measure to the hem line *Note.* These three measurements are taken simultaneously, and all three from the shoulder	—
16	Width at waist	Taken loosely at the level indicated by the waist tape	—
6	Width at hip	Taken very loosely at the hip tape	—

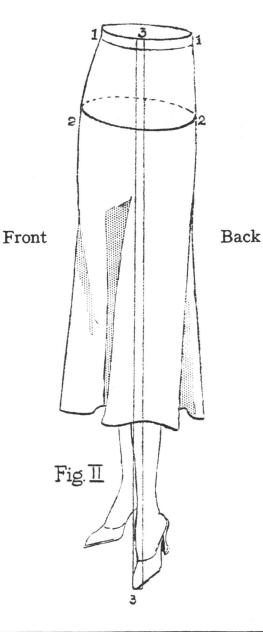

Front

Back

Fig. II

Skirt Measurements.

A separate skirt is usually mounted on a Petersham waist band, and the waist line is therefore above the natural waist line of the figure.

To get an accurate measurement pin the Petersham round the waist and take the waist measurement at the top edge of the band.

If the Petersham is not available pin a tape round the waist at the correct level according to the width of band which is to be used.

No.	Measurement	Method of Taking	Average Size
			in.
1	Waist	Measured loosely at the top edge of waist band	30
2	Hip	Taken very loosely 7 in. below the lowest edge of waist band (the natural waist line)	40
3	Length . . .	Taken from the top edge of waist band at side seam to the floor, and the desired amount subtracted.	—

CHAPTER III

BLOCK PATTERN

Jumper Pattern. Fig. III.

CONSTRUCTION LINES

AB	Nape to hip measure $+ \frac{1}{2}$ in. ruled down left side of paper.
AA^2	$\frac{1}{4}$ width of hip $+ 2$ in. ruled to right of A. (Neck line.)
A^2B^2	Parallel and equal to AB.
BB^2	Parallel and equal to AA^2. (Hip line.)
AC	Nape to waist measure $+ \frac{1}{2}$ in. Rule CC^2. (Waist line.)
AD	$\frac{1}{2} AC$. Rule DD^2. (Bust line.)
AE	$\frac{1}{2} AD$. Rule EE^2. (Chest line).

Jumper Block Pattern.

Fig. III

MEASUREMENTS		
		in.
Nape to waist	. .	$15\frac{1}{2}$
Nape to hip .	. .	$22\frac{1}{2}$
Width of bust	.	36
Width of back	.	12
Width of chest	.	14
Width of hip .	. .	40
Shoulder length	. .	5

PATTERN LINES. BACK

AF	$\frac{1}{2}$ in.
AG	$2\frac{1}{4}$ in. ($2\frac{1}{2}$ in. if bust measurement is over 38 in.). Curve FG.
CH	$\frac{1}{4}$ in. Rule F through H to hip line. This is now the centre back line of pattern.

7

EI	$\frac{1}{2}$ width of back $+ \frac{1}{2}$ in.
IJ	Half-way between I and neck line. Rule GJ and **extend if neces-** sary to the length of shoulder (5 in.).
K	$\frac{1}{4}$ bust measure less $\frac{1}{2}$ in. measured to right of centre back line on the bust line. Curve from J through I to K.
L	$\frac{1}{4}$ hip measure less 1 in. measured to right of centre back line on the hip line. Rule KL.

Front

A^3	Raise the front neck line 1 in. ($1\frac{1}{2}$ in. to 2 in. for larger bust measurements).
A^3F^2	3 in.
A^3G^2	$2\frac{3}{4}$ in. Draw a construction line from G^2 to F^2 and mark centre. Rule from A^3 through this centre point and 1 in. lower. Curve from G^2 through the end of this line to F^2.
H^2	$\frac{1}{4}$ in. to right of C^2. Rule from F^2 through H^2 to the hip line. (This is now centre front line.)
E^2I^2	$\frac{1}{2}$ width of chest $+ \frac{1}{2}$ in. Rule a construction line from G^2 to E. Measure from G^2 the shoulder length measurement and mark a point.
J^2	$\frac{1}{2}$ in. below this point. Rule G^2J^2.
K^2	$\frac{1}{4}$ bust $+ 1\frac{1}{2}$ in. to left of centre front line on the bust line. Mark a guiding point $1\frac{1}{2}$ in. to right of K^2. Draw armhole curve from J^2 through I^2 and this guiding point to K^2.
L^2	$\frac{1}{4}$ hip $+ 1$ in. to left of centre front line on the hip line. Rule K^2L^2.

Sleeve Pattern. Fig. IV.

Construction Lines

AB	Length of sleeve ruled down left edge of paper.
AA^2	Width of sleeve ruled to right of A.
A^2B^2	Parallel and equal to AB.
BB^2	Parallel and equal to AA^2.
CC^2	Half-way between AB and A^2B^2.
AD	$\frac{1}{3}$ armhole measurement. Rule DD^2. Rule DC and D^2C.

Pattern Lines

DE	$\frac{1}{3}DC$.
D^2F	$\frac{1}{2}D^2C$. Curve as in Diagram. Deepest part of curve between D and E is about $\frac{1}{4}$ in. Deepest part of curve between E and C is about $\frac{3}{4}$ in. Deepest part of curve between C and F is about $\frac{1}{2}$ in. Deepest part of curve between F and D^2 is about $\frac{1}{2}$ in.
BG	$1\frac{1}{2}$ in. Rule DG and find centre point.
B^2G^2	$1\frac{1}{4}$ in. Rule D^2G^2 and find centre point.

H	$\frac{1}{2}$ in. to right of centre of DG. Curve from D through H to G.
H^2	$\frac{1}{2}$ in. to left of centre of D^2G^2. Curve from D^2 through H^2 to G^2.
G^2I	$\frac{1}{3}$ of GG^2. Curve as in diagram from G through I to G^2. The deepest part of the curve between G and I is about $\frac{1}{2}$ in., and between I and G^2 about $\frac{1}{4}$ in.

Note : The seam of this sleeve is set about $\frac{3}{4}$ in. in front of under-arm seam.

Blouse Sleeve.

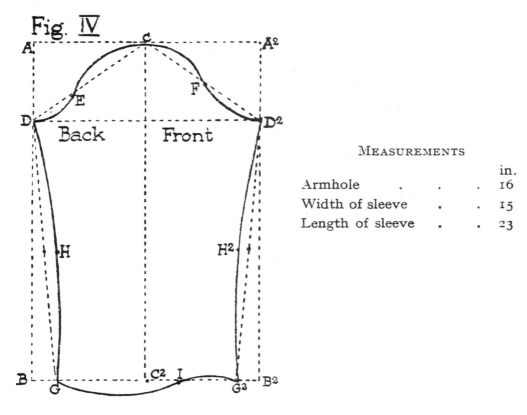

Fig. IV

MEASUREMENTS

	in.
Armhole . . .	16
Width of sleeve . .	15
Length of sleeve . .	23

Explanatory Notes on Some of the Points of the Jumper Block.

It may be desirable to explain some of the points of the draft for the benefit of the more thoughtful student who is not prepared to accept the measurements given without some further explanation.

AB and AC	The added $\frac{1}{2}$ in. to the length measure allows for the curve of the neck from F to G.
H and H^2	It has been found that the sloping forward of the centre back and centre front line gives a better balance to the bodice and prevents the poke forward at the front that sometimes happens.
AG	This was given formerly as $\frac{1}{6}$ of the width of back. The difference was so fractional that it seemed simpler to give the measurement as $2\frac{1}{4}$ in. for average figures and $2\frac{1}{2}$ in. for larger measurements.

A^3F^2 and A^3G^2	For the reason given above it seemed easier to give an arbitrary measurement as the difference was so infinitesimal in the different measurements.
I and I^2	$\frac{1}{2}$ in. is added to the actual measurement to give ease in fitting.
K and K^2	The bust measure is used in fixing these points. The back of the bodice should obviously be narrower in width than the front. If a perfectly tight fitting bodice is required the correct division of the bust measure is $\frac{1}{4}$ of the bust measure less 1 in. at the back, and $\frac{1}{4}$ of the bust measure $+$ 1 in. at the front. This gives the correct proportion.

In this pattern $\frac{1}{2}$ in. extra is allowed for ease both at back and front, therefore K is measured to the right of centre back $\frac{1}{4}$ bust less 1 in. $+$ $\frac{1}{2}$ in. for ease ($\frac{1}{4}$ bust less $\frac{1}{2}$ in.).

For the same reason K^2 is measured to the left of the centre front line $\frac{1}{4}$ bust $+$ 1 in. $+$ $\frac{1}{2}$ in. for ease ($\frac{1}{4}$ bust $+$ $1\frac{1}{2}$ in.).

L and L^2	The same ruling applies for these points as for K and K^2, with the difference that no extra width is allowed for, as the average jumper fits closely to the figure at the hip.
A^3	Raising the front neck line gives the extra length necessary to allow the jumper to fit over the bust in front. The amount allowed depends on the figure—a very large figure may require still more length, which may be obtained by curving the hip and waist lines downward in front, but this should be avoided if possible.

CHAPTER IV

SKIRT CUTTING

MOST skirts may be said to flare outwards from the waist to the hem, the fashion of the moment regulating the amount of the flare.

A very simple and straightforward method of obtaining a flare is shown here and the method of adapting this to the particular skirt required.

The method of taking skirt measurements has already been explained.

The absolutely essential measurements are—

      1. Waist: Stock size 30 in.
      2. Hip: ,,   ,, 40 in.
      3. Length: ,,   ,, 30 in.

It may be necessary to know the approximate width at the hem.

The cutter will do well to bear in mind that 54 in. is the average width for a fairly narrow walking skirt. It may be wider and it is sometimes fashionable to have skirts cut narrower than that, but a narrower skirt does not give freedom for walking easily. The hem of a pleated skirt should be from 45 in. to 54 in. exclusive of the pleats.

It must be emphasized once more that the waist and hip measurements are taken very loosely.

The waist measurement is taken at the top of the waist band and the length measurements are also taken from that level.

The skirt is always drafted in one piece from front to back, and is afterwards divided up into its different parts.

In all the skirts shown the stock measurements are used.

Skirt 1. (Fig. V) Flared Skirt.

This skirt fits the waist and hip, and continues in the natural line to the hem, thus giving a considerable width at the bottom edge.

The pattern is worked out in two "Movements."

1ST MOVEMENT (Fig. V (a))

AB	Length of skirt. (Centre back line.)
AA^2	$\frac{1}{4}$ waist measure. (Waist line.)
A^2B^2	Parallel and equal to AB. (Centre front line.)
BB^2	Parallel and equal to AA^2. (Hem line.)
AC	9 in. (i.e. the width of waist band, 2 in. + the space between the natural waist and hip lines, 7 in.).
	Rule CC^2. (Hip line.)

The "pattern" as it is now is correct in length and correct in width at the waist line, but is not sufficiently wide at the hip and hem.

2ND MOVEMENT (Fig. V (b))

Cut out the "pattern" and divide into 8 equal sections, as shown in Fig. V(a).
Cut along the dividing lines from the hem line to $\frac{1}{8}$ in. of the waist line.

Pin the pattern to another sheet of paper, keeping A^2B^2 straight with the right hand edge of the paper but spreading out the sections so that CC^2 is extended to the $\frac{1}{2}$ hip measure. (Add 1 in. if a looser hip is desired.)

Skirt 1.

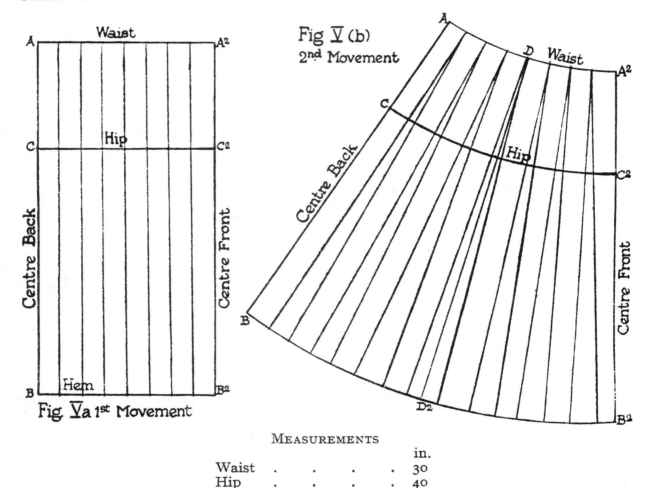

Fig. V a 1st Movement

Fig V (b) 2nd Movement

MEASUREMENTS

	in.
Waist	30
Hip	40
Length	30

It is essential that great care is taken in measuring the hip curve. Measure with a tape round the curve.

The sections must be spaced equally and the waist line must lie perfectly flat.

Outline the pattern thus obtained and mark in the hip line.

The skirt now fits at waist and hip and is approximately $1\frac{3}{4}$ yd. at hem.

It may be divided into gores according to the style required.

The diagram shows the skirt divided into two equal parts by DD^2. (Side seam.)

Skirt. 2. (Fig. VI.) **Costume Skirt of Average Width.**

The average costume skirt fits rather loosely at the hip and is about 54 in. wide at the hem.

It will be seen that the pattern for SKIRT I is not suitable as the hem is too wide.

The hip line may not be reduced, therefore the hip measurement is the dominating measure on which to base the draft.

1ST MOVEMENT (Fig. VI (a))

AB	Length of skirt (centre back line).
AA^2	$\frac{1}{2}$ hip measurement $+$ 1 in. (Waist line.)
A^2B^2	Equal and parallel to AB. (Centre front line.)
BB^2	Equal and parallel to AA^2. (Hem line.)
AC	9 in. (Hip level.) Rule CC^2. (Hip line.)

The " pattern " now fits loosely at the hip and is correct in length, but must be reduced at the top edge to fit the waist and widened at the bottom edge to the desired width of hem.

2ND MOVEMENT (Fig. VI (b))

Cut out the pattern.

Divide the width into 8 equal sections as in Fig. VI (a).

Cut along the dividing lines from the hem up to $\frac{1}{8}$ in. of the *hip line*, and from the waist down to $\frac{1}{8}$ in. of the *hip line*.

Place the pattern on another sheet of paper with A^2B^2 straight with the right-hand edge of the paper. Spread out the sections below the hip line so that BB^2 is extended to 27 in. (or half the desired width at hem). The sections above the hip line will slightly overwrap each other, thus somewhat reducing the width of the waist line.

Outline the pattern and mark in the hip line.

The pattern is now the required width at the hip and at the hem, but the waist line, if measured, will be found to be still too wide.

Fig. VI (b) shows the method of reducing the width at the waist by means of a dart.

The skirt has been divided into a two-piece skirt, and as much as possible of the extra width at waist has been taken away by means of a dart at the top of the side seam.

The remainder of the fulness could be eased into the waist band across the back or could be taken out in smaller darts or tucks at the back.

A^2D	$\frac{1}{2} AA^2$ less 1 in.
C^2E	$\frac{1}{2} CC^2$ less 1 in. Rule from D through E to the hem line. (Side seam.)
	Measure AA^2. In the pattern shown here this is 19 in. Subtract from this the $\frac{1}{2}$ waist measure, 15 in. The surplus width at waist is, therefore, 19 in. $-$ 15 in. $=$ 4 in. Some of this may be taken out in a dart

at the top of the side seam, but the hip line must not be altered, and the line of the seam must not be spoilt, therefore, the dart may not be too wide.

DF and $1\frac{1}{4}$ in. Curve very carefully from these points to *E*, keeping straight
DF²   below the waist line for about 2 in., and then curving gradually
          outwards till the two lines meet about 1 in. above *E*.

     Thus a dart of $2\frac{1}{2}$ in. is taken out at the side seam and the remaining $1\frac{1}{2}$ in. surplus width may be dealt with as explained above.

Skirt 2.   2ND MOVEMENT

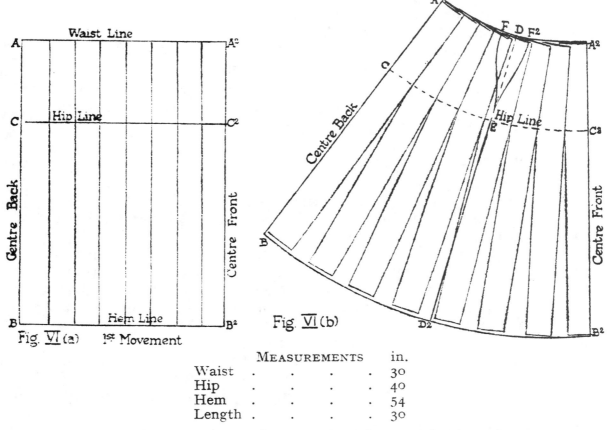

Fig. VI (a)   1ˢᵗ Movement   Fig. VI (b)

MEASUREMENTS	in.
Waist	30
Hip	40
Hem	54
Length	30

Note : The division of the width of this skirt, making the front narrower than the back, appears to contradict the statements made elsewhere in this book on the proportions of the front and back.

Below the waist the figure is narrower in front than at the back, therefore the side seam of a separate skirt is placed 1 in. nearer the front, but if an entire dress is being made the seam of the skirt usually follows in a line with the seam of the bodice, and is nearer the back.

Skirt 3. (Fig. VII.) Skirt with Fitted Hip Yoke and Flared Lower Part.

This skirt is cut on the same lines as Skirt I, but has a hip yoke, and the lower part of the skirt is still further flared.

Skirt 3.

1ST AND 2ND MOVEMENTS AS IN SKIRT 1.

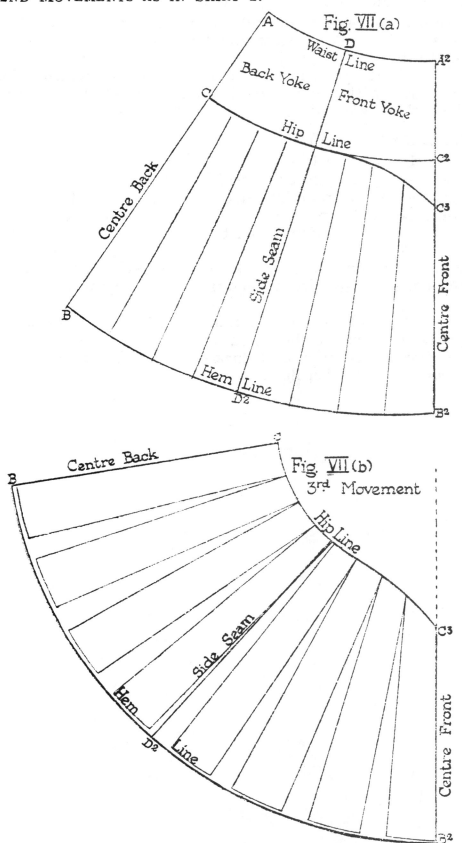

Fig. VII (a)

A
Waist Line
D
A²
Back Yoke
Front Yoke
C
Hip Line
C²
C³
Centre Back
Side Seam
Centre Front
B
Hem Line
D²
B²

Fig. VII (b)
3rd Movement

Centre Back
B
Hip Line
C³
Side Seam
Hem
D²
Line
Centre Front
B²

1ST AND 2ND MOVEMENTS (Fig. VII (*a*))

Proceed as for Skirt 1, and rule in the side seam.

The skirt now fits at waist and hip, therefore the yoke pattern may be taken from this.

The line of the yoke may, of course, be varied with one or more points, or it may be a perfectly straight line on the level of the normal hip line. It must be outlined and cut away from the main pattern.

3RD MOVEMENT (Fig. VII (*b*))

Divide the lower part of the skirt into 8 equal parts. Cut up these sections from the hem line to $\frac{1}{8}$ in. from the hip line.

Place the centre front line straight with the right-hand edge of another sheet of paper and spread out the sections to make a still wider flare. The spaces between the sections must be equal; the width is regulated according to the style of the skirt.

To make the skirt hem form a complete circle, spread out the sections so that the side seam is horizontal and the centre back is in a line with the centre front.

The skirt shown in the diagram is about $2\frac{3}{4}$ yd. in width. The spaces between the sections are about 2 in. wide.

This gives a good flare for a thick material, but a thin silk or georgette may be cut with a much fuller flare.

Skirt 4.

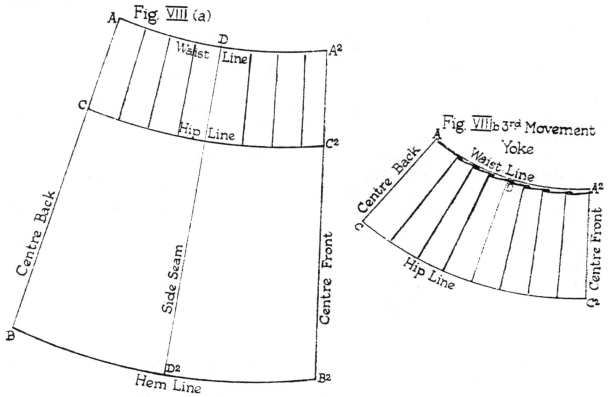

Fig. VIII (a)

Fig. VIIIb 3rd Movement Yoke

Skirt 4. Yoked Skirt with Hem 54 in. Wide. (Fig. VIII.)

This skirt is cut on the same lines as Skirt 2, but as the yoke is cut separately it can be shaped to fit exactly at the waist without darts or fulness.

1ST AND 2ND MOVEMENTS (Fig. VIII (*a*))

Proceed as for Skirt 2, and rule in the side seam.

Draw in the line of the hip yoke as desired. In the diagram, Fig. VIII (*a*), the yoke is cut on the actual hip line, but it may be shaped in any way desired, as described in Skirt 3.

The lower part of the skirt is correct in width at both hem and hip lines and is left unaltered.

3RD MOVEMENT (Fig. VIII (*b*))

Cut away the upper part of pattern above the hip line.

Divide into 8 equal sections and cut along the divisions from the *waist line* down to ⅛ in. of *hip line*.

The hip line is correct as to measurement, but the waist line has to be reduced.

Place the centre front of the pattern at the right-hand edge of another piece of paper and overlap the sections at the top edges so that the waist is reduced to the desired width. (½ waist measure.)

Outline the pattern thus obtained and rule in the side seam, taking care that it follows the line of seam of the lower part of skirt. Fig. VIII (*b*).

CHAPTER V

ADAPTATION OF BLOCK PATTERN

ONE hesitates about making any definite statements on pattern cutting, knowing that they will be contradicted as fashions and ideas alter, but a very few general rules may be ventured on.

Before attempting to adapt the block pattern the cutter must study the sketch she is copying very closely and note all the points of difference.

A dress usually fits fairly loosely across the bust, therefore, in drafting the block pattern ½ in. has already been added for ease at the bust line of both back and front of pattern. It may be necessary to add still more.

The present-day dresses fit the hip rather closely; therefore, though care must be taken to allow sufficient width in measuring, no extra ease is allowed on the pattern as a rule.

The waist may or may not be close-fitting.

Placing the Block Pattern.

It will be seen that in all the adaptations a similar procedure is followed in placing the block pattern on the paper.

The front is placed first with the centre front line absolutely straight.

The back is then placed with the centre back line absolutely straight, but also it must have the hip line at the same level as the hip line of the front.

If the hip line is not horizontal make sure that at least the lowest point of the under-arm seam at back and front are in a line.

This is absolutely essential, as in all cases the adaptation is worked out as a whole pattern, the same set of construction lines serving for both back and front.

Proportion of Width Measurements.

In dividing the all-round width measurements, i.e. the bust, waist and hip, they are divided unequally between the back and front of the pattern in this proportion—

At back: from centre back to under-arm seam, allow ¼ width less 1 in.

At front: from centre front to under-arm seam, allow ¼ width + 1 in.

Width of Skirt at Hem.

There is practically no limit to the width of skirt at the hem, but the narrowest skirt which allows for freedom in walking is 45 in. to 54 in., preferably the latter.

A pleated skirt should have the pleats in excess of this.

Shoulder Darts.

To ensure an easy fit over the bust and also a closer fit at the arm-hole, it is nearly always desirable when using the block pattern to make a dart or pleats on the shoulder.

This could be allowed for in drafting, but as the amount allowed varies according to the style, it is considered preferable to make alterations in the adaptation as required.

Neck Line.

It is usually the safer course to cut the neck by the line of the block pattern, and to make the desired alteration when fitting.

Testing Pattern.

The adaptation having been worked out as a whole and the style lines marked in, it is wise to cut the back and front of pattern in outline only. This can be held against the figure, and the style lines can then be judged both as regards to general "line," and also as to their suitability for that particular figure.

Any alterations may then be made before cutting up the pattern into its various parts.

Marking Pattern.

Before cutting out the pattern write any necessary instructions on it which will help in planning out the material and in putting the garment together.

Mark clearly the centre back and front of each part, and state if placed to a fold or selvedge.

The corresponding points of contact should be marked with notches; one notch for the first seam, two for the second, and so on.

Explanation of the Diagrams.

The red lines of the diagrams show the original block pattern.
Dotted red lines indicate the construction lines.
Black lines indicate the finished pattern as it is to be cut.

CHAPTER VI

BLOUSES

General Instructions which will Not be Repeated in Subsequent Adaptations.

IF in adapting the pattern, the lines of the block pattern are drawn in red, and those of the adaptation itself in black pencil, mistakes in cutting out the final pattern will be avoided.

Fig. IX clearly shows the arrangement of the block pattern on the new sheet of paper preparatory to making the adaptation. The paper is represented by black dotted lines; in subsequent diagrams this will be omitted.

Red lines represent the block pattern.

Black lines represent the finished adaptation.

In most of the adaptations shown in this book the some procedure is followed as in Blouse I as regards making the necessary pleat or tucks on the shoulder and placing the block pattern on the paper. The instruction will not, therefore, be repeated.

Blouse 1. (Fig. IX.)

POINTS TO BE NOTED IN THE DESIGN

THE blouse is pouched at the waist; therefore, about 3 in. extra length must be allowed below the natural waist line.

The design shows a dart on the shoulder.

An inset vest extends to a distance of about 2 in. above the natural waist line. This appears in the sketch to be about 3 in. wide at the neck and widens to about 5 in. at the widest part.

METHOD OF ADAPTATION

Place the front of the block pattern on a new sheet of paper with the centre front at the right-hand edge of the paper.

Mark the line of the shoulder pleat (about the centre of the shoulder).

Remove the block and pin in the shoulder pleat on the paper. This is about $\frac{3}{4}$ in. wide at the shoulder and tapers off to about $\frac{3}{8}$ in. It is 6 in. or 7 in. long. The pleat slopes very slightly forward.

Pin the front of the block pattern in position again, keeping the centre front exactly at the right-hand edge of the paper and allowing the fulness caused by the pleat to lie under the pattern across the bust, but avoid any fulness at the hip line.

Pin on the back of the block pattern so that the hip line is level with that of the front, and the centre back line is vertical.

Outline the two parts of the pattern and remove the block. Mark in waist line.

Blouse 1.

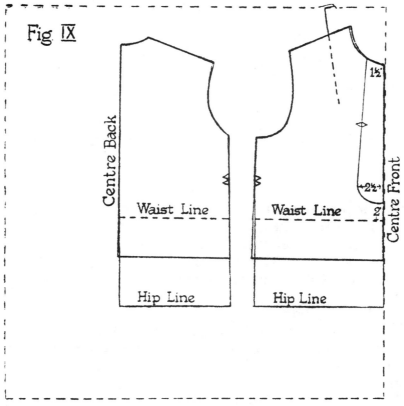

Fig. IX

Centre Back

Waist Line   Waist Line

Centre Front

1½"

2½"

2

Hip Line   Hip Line

Fig. IX

The pattern is now similar to the block pattern with the addition of fulness at the shoulder. Draw in the line of the vest following the lines of the design, as noted above.

Rule in the new waist line 3 in. below that of the block pattern.

Blouse 2. (Fig. X.)

This is a standard pattern which with some slight modification is always in vogue.

Points to be Noted

The blouse is pouched at the waist and probably requires 3 in. in length below the natural waist line.

The gathered front is set into a shoulder strap. The shoulder strap appears to be about 2 in. below the shoulder in front, and probably 1 in. at the back.

There is no extra fulness at the back.

Method of Adaptation

Pin the block pattern on the paper in correct position, allowing $2\frac{1}{2}$ in. between the centre front of block and the right-hand edge of the paper. This is for the front fulness.

Pencil round block pattern and remove.

AB (Front edge of shoulder strap.) 2 in. below the shoulder seam in front and ruled parallel to it.

CD (Back edge of shoulder strap.) 1 in. below the shoulder seam at back and ruled parallel to it.

B^2 Measured horizontally to the right of B $2\frac{1}{2}$ in. (the amount of material allowed for fulness).

Rule AB^2.

Rule in a new centre front line $2\frac{1}{2}$ in. (or the same amount as BB^2) to right of the original one and curve for the front neck from B^2.

Rule in waist line 3 in. below the natural waist line at back and front.

To avoid having too much fulness at the waist the under-arm seam may be sloped forward about $1\frac{1}{2}$ in.

Note : As a blouse of this type frequently has a front fastening, Fig. X shows method of cutting (the shaded part at centre front of the diagram).

This allows for a box pleat in front $1\frac{1}{2}$ in. wide when finished.

It is better not to curve the neck line until the box pleat is made.

Fig. X (*b*). Shoulder Strap

Place the back and front of block pattern together at the shoulder line as shown in the diagram. Trace off the shoulder strap in one piece (*A, B, C, D*). The edges of the shoulder strap should be clearly marked: front edge, back edge, arm-hole and neck, as a mistake is very easily made in attaching the shoulder strap to the blouse.

Blouse 2 (with Shoulder Strap and Fulness on Shoulder).

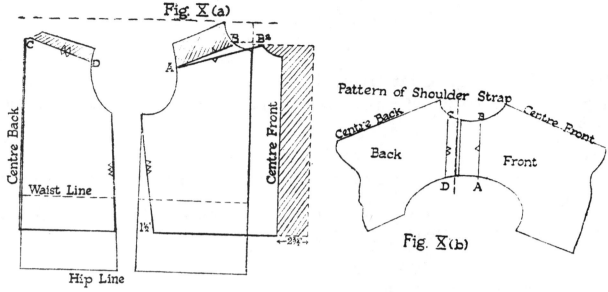

The shaded part at front edge shows method of cutting if a front fastening is required. This gives a box pleat 1½ in. when finished.

Fig. X

CHAPTER VII

DRESSES

Dress 1. (Fig. XI.) Coat Overall.

THIS is the simplest type of full-length garment which can be adapted from the block pattern.

POINTS TO BE NOTED

The pattern has a dart in front shoulder and has a 2 in. overwrap to allow for front fastening.

In making the garment the front edge will probably be faced back, as indicated by black dotted lines in diagram.

EXTRA MEASUREMENTS NECESSARY

Front shoulder to hem: 45 in.
Width at hem: 54 in.

METHOD OF ADAPTATION

Centre front line. Rule a line 2 in. in from the right-hand edge of paper. The 2 in. allows for overwrap and is left on the pattern.

Make the necessary shoulder pleat in the paper and pin on the front of the block pattern with the centre front straight with the line just drawn.

Hip line. Ruled across the paper at the same level as the hip line of the block pattern, and at a right angle to centre front line.

Centre back line. Measure on the hip line from the centre front line the half-width of hem (27 in.). At that distance from the front line and parallel to it rule the centre back line.

Pin on the back of the block pattern with the hip line and centre back level with the lines just drawn.

Outline the block pattern and remove.

Hem line. Measure from the highest point of the front shoulder the shoulder to hem measurement. At this level rule a line across the paper.

Continue the centre back and centre front lines to touch the hem line.

AB $\frac{1}{4}$ width of hem, less 1 in.
CB^2 $\frac{1}{4}$ width of hem + 1 in.

Side seams. Rule from the under-arm points at back and front to B and B^2.

Curve the hem slightly upwards at B and B^2 to avoid a point at the end of the seam.

Draw in the front neck curve about $\frac{3}{4}$ in. higher than that of the block pattern, and continue to edge of the overwrap.

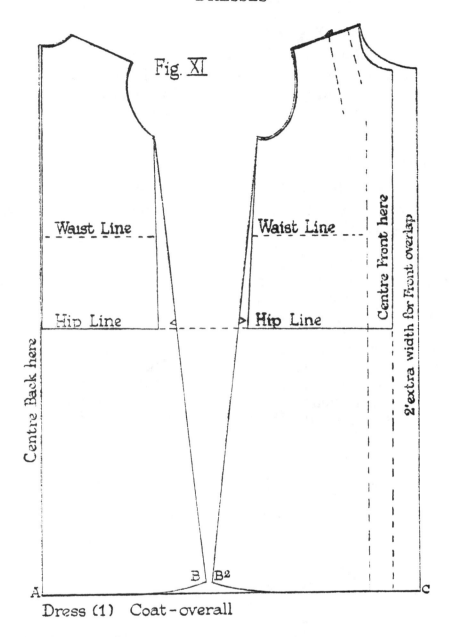

Fig. XI

Waist Line

Hip Line

Centre Back here

Waist Line

Hip Line

Centre Front here

2' extra width for Front overlap

A   B B²   C

Dress (1)   Coat-overall

Dress 2. (Fig. XII.)   Dress with Skirt Flared from Waist.

POINTS TO BE NOTED

The bodice is apparently fitted in to the natural waist line. A dart or pleat is probably necessary at the front shoulder. The skirt flares outwards from the waist but appears to fit at the hip.

MEASUREMENTS NECESSARY

Pin tapes round the natural waist and hip lines.

Front shoulder to waist,	17 in.	Width at waist, 28 in.
Front shoulder to hip,	24 in.	Width at hip, 40 in.
Front shoulder to hem,	45 in.	(Take width measurements very loosely.)

METHOD OF ADAPTATION

The pattern is worked out in two "movements."

1. The bodice is adapted and the foundation of the skirt prepared.
2. Flared skirt.

1ST MOVEMENT. Fig. XII (*a*)

Pin the front and back of block pattern on the paper as described in Blouse 1, Fig. IX, allowing for pleat on·the front shoulder.

Outline block pattern and remove.

Measure down from the highest point of front shoulder:

(*a*) Shoulder to waist measure. Rule waist line.
(*b*) Shoulder to hip measure. Rule hip line.
(*c*) Shoulder to hem measure. Rule hem line.

Continue centre back and centre front lines to meet hem line.

AB $\qquad$ $\frac{1}{4}$ waist, less 1 in.
A^2B^2 $\qquad$ $\frac{1}{4}$ waist $+$ 1 in.

Mark C and C^2 the under-arm points of back and front.

Rule BC and B^2C^2.

Rule vertical lines from B and B^2 to hem line.

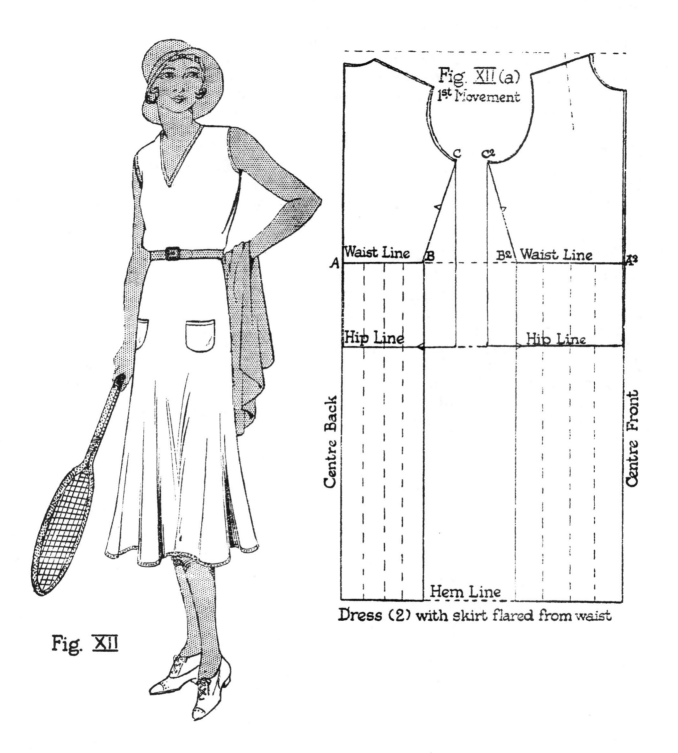

Fig. XII

Fig. XII (a)
1st Movement

Waist Line B   B² Waist Line
A   A²

Hip Line   Hip Line

Centre Back

Centre Front

Hem Line

Dress (2) with skirt flared from waist

2ND MOVEMENT. Fig. XII (*b*)

Cut away the two parts of the skirt below the waist line. Note that the hip line is clearly marked, also centre front and back.

If put together the skirt would now be correct in length and the waist would be correct, but there is not sufficient width at hip line and hem.

Divide both back and front of skirt into 4 equal sections. Cut up the divisions from the hem line to $\frac{1}{8}$ in. of waist.

BACK OF SKIRT

Place centre back to the left-hand edge of a new sheet of paper, and spread out the sections so that the hip line is extended to $\frac{1}{4}$ hip measure less 1 in.

The sections must be equally spaced, and the pattern must lie flat on the paper.

Outline the pattern thus obtained.

FRONT OF SKIRT

Place centre front to the right-hand edge of paper. Spread out the sections so that the hip line is extended to $\frac{1}{4}$ hip + 1 in.

Outline the pattern.

It will be seen that the measurement of the waist line is not altered, so will fit on to the waist line of the bodice when the skirt is joined to the bodice.

The skirt may not be any narrower in width or it would not fit the hip line, but it may be wider if desired.

To obtain a wider skirt spread out the sections to the desired width.

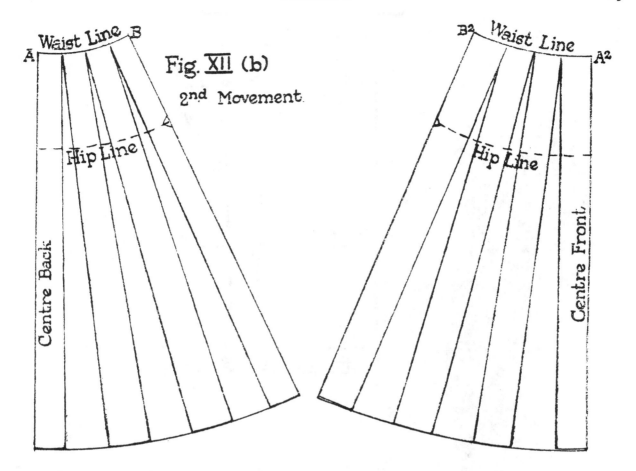

Fig. XII (b)

2nd Movement

Waist Line B

A

Hip Line

Centre Back

B2 Waist Line

A2

Hip Line

Centre Front

Dress 3. (Fig. XIII.) With Skirt Flared from the Hip Line.

POINTS TO BE NOTED:

The bodice of this dress is cut in one piece from shoulder to hip, the waist line being defined by the belt.

The hip line appears to be rather lower than the natural hip line and curves down to a point in front. The skirt is only slightly flared below the hip line. The shoulder fulness is arranged in two small tucks.

MEASUREMENTS NECESSARY

Pin a tape round the hips about $1\frac{1}{2}$ in. lower than the natural hip line or at the level which best suits the wearer of the dress.

Front shoulder to hip: $25\frac{1}{2}$ in.   Width at hip: 42 in.
Front shoulder to hem: 45 in.

METHOD OF ADAPTATION

As in Dress 2, Fig. XII, the pattern for this dress is worked out in two movements.

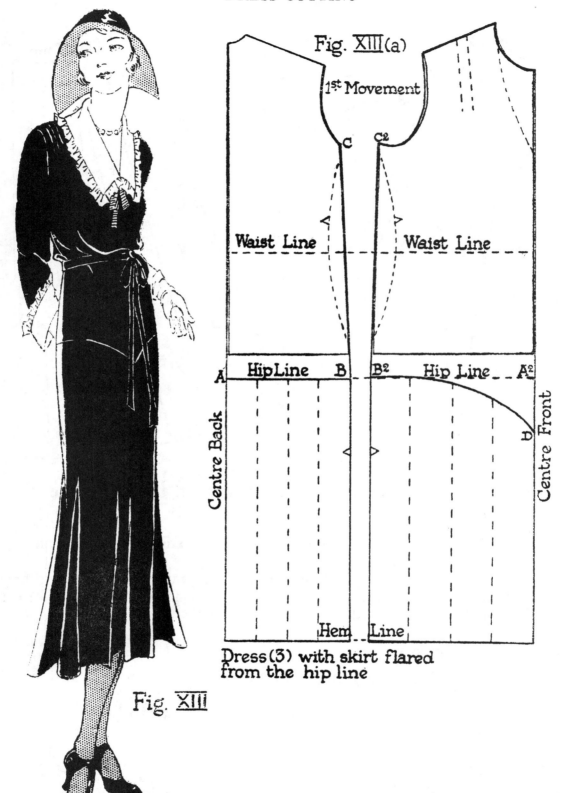

Fig. XIII(a)

1st Movement

C   C²

Waist Line   Waist Line

A   Hip Line   B   B²   Hip Line   A²

Centre Back   Centre Front

D

Hem   Line

Dress (3) with skirt flared
from the hip line

Fig. XIII

1ST MOVEMENT. Fig. XIII (*a*)

Proceed as for Dress 2, Fig. XII, allowing for two small tucks on the shoulder instead of a pleat.

Outline block pattern and remove.

Measure down from the front shoulder.

(*a*) Shoulder to hip.   Rule hip line.
(*b*) Shoulder to hem.   Rule hem line.

Continue centre back and centre front lines to touch hem line.

AB $\frac{1}{4}$ hip less 1 in.

A^2B^2 $\frac{1}{4}$ hip + 1 in.

          Rule BC and B^2C^2 as in diagram, but if a closer fit is desired at the waist the under-arm seam may be curved slightly inwards at the waist line. A sharp angle at the hip and under-arm points must be avoided.

A^2D Apparently about 3 in. Curve the front hip line down to a point at D.

          Rule vertical lines from B and B^2 to hem line.

2ND MOVEMENT. Fig. XIII (*b*)

Cut away the two parts of the skirt; cutting along the line from A to B and from B^2 to D.

Divide both parts into 4 equal sections as for Dress 2, Fig. XII.

Place centre back to left-hand edge of paper, and centre front to right-hand edge, and open out the sections so that there is a space of about 2 in. between each section.

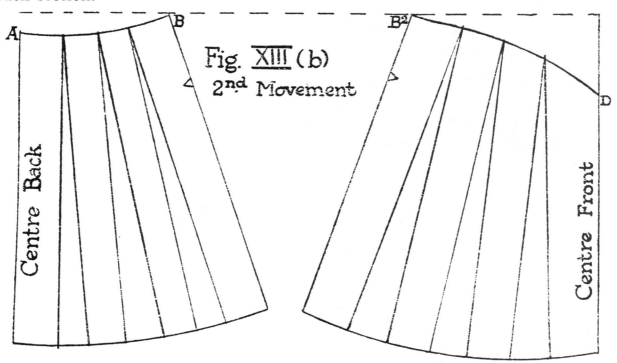

Fig. XIII (b)
2nd Movement

Outline pattern thus obtained.

This only gives a width of about 54 in. at the hem. If a wider flare is desired spread out the sections still further, but they must be evenly spread, and the hip line must not be altered in measurement.

Dress 4. (Fig. XIV.)   Dress with Hip Yoke and Flared Skirt.

POINTS TO BE NOTED

The bodice is set on to a hip yoke and is slightly pouched at the waist.
The shoulder has 3 small inverted tucks.
The hip yoke fits to the natural waist line—the hip line (the lower edge of yoke) is somewhat lower than the natural hip line.
The skirt flares outwards from the hip line, but is not apparently very full at the hem.

EXTRA MEASUREMENTS NECESSARY

Pin tapes round the natural waist line and about 2 in. below the natural hip line (or at the level at which the wearer desires the hip yoke to terminate).

Shoulder to waist:	17 in.	Width at waist:	28 in.
Shoulder to hip:	26 in.	Width at hip:	42 in.
Shoulder to hem:	45 in.		

METHOD OF ADAPTATION

The pattern is worked out in 3 movements:
1. Adaptation of bodice and skirt foundation.
2. Hip yoke and foundation of flare.
3. Flared skirt.

1ST MOVEMENT. Fig. XIV (*a*)

Place the block pattern on paper as before, except that in this case 3 small tucks are pinned in the paper to give shoulder fulness.
Outline pattern and remove.
Measure down from the front shoulder:

Shoulder to waist.	Rule waist line.
Shoulder to hip.	Rule hip line.
Shoulder to hem.	Rule hem line.

Continue centre back and centre front lines to hem line.

AB $\frac{1}{4}$ waist, less 1 in.
A^2B^2 $\frac{1}{4}$ waist + 1 in.
       Rule vertical lines from B and B^2 to the hem line
C and C^2 $\frac{3}{4}$ in. outside B and B^2 (extra width at the waist of the bodice to allow for ease.
       Rule CD and C^2D^2 (under-arm seams) as in diagram.

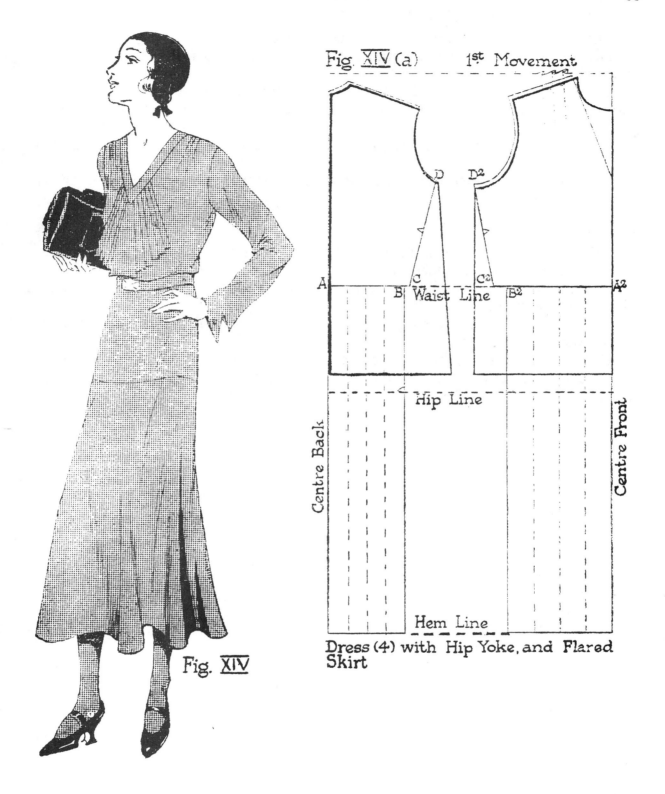

Fig. XIV (a)   1st Movement

Waist Line

Hip Line

Centre Back

Centre Front

Hem Line

Dress (4) with Hip Yoke, and Flared Skirt

Fig. XIV

2ND MOVEMENT. Fig. XIV (*b*)

Cut away the back and front of the skirt.

Divide both parts into 4 equal sections and cut up from the hem to $\frac{1}{8}$ in. of waist line.

Proceed as for Dress 2, Fig. XII(*b*), spreading out the sections of both back and front so that the hip line at back equals $\frac{1}{4}$ hip, less 1 in., and at front, $\frac{1}{4}$ hip + 1 in.

Outline the two parts of the pattern, taking care to have a good line at the hip line.

Cut away the upper part (the hip yoke pattern). Mark centre front and back carefully.

3RD MOVEMENT

The lower part of the skirt may be left as it is or it may be extended to a wider flare by a similar method.

Divide the two parts into 4 equal sections and cut from the hem to $\frac{1}{8}$ in. of hip line. Fig. XIV(*c*).

Place the centre back to the left-hand edge of a third sheet of paper, and spread out the sections to give the required flare. Fig. XIV (*d*).

Obtain the front of the skirt pattern by the same method. The spaces between the sections must be equal—in the diagram a 2 in. space is allowed, and this makes a skirt of about 3 yd. in width at the hem.

2nd Movement

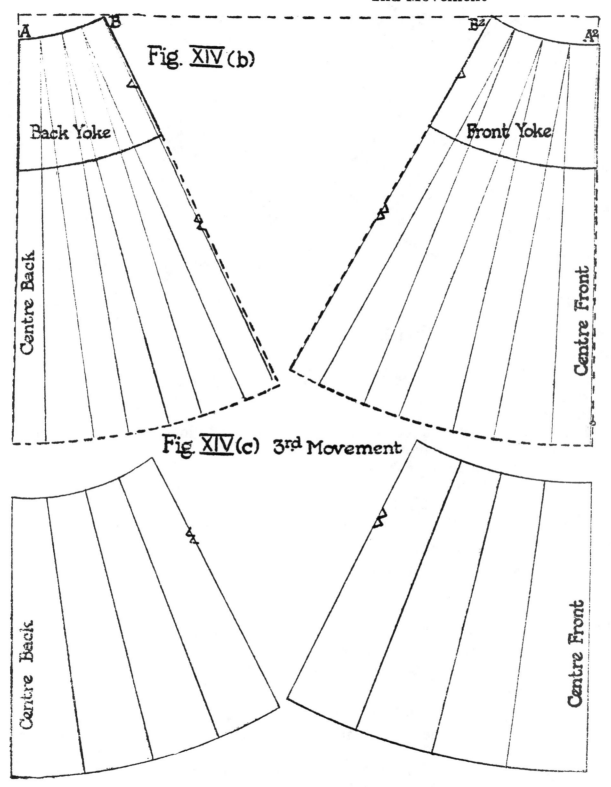

Fig. XIV (b)

Back Yoke

Centre Back

Front Yoke

Centre Front

Fig. XIV (c) 3rd Movement

Centre Back

Centre Front

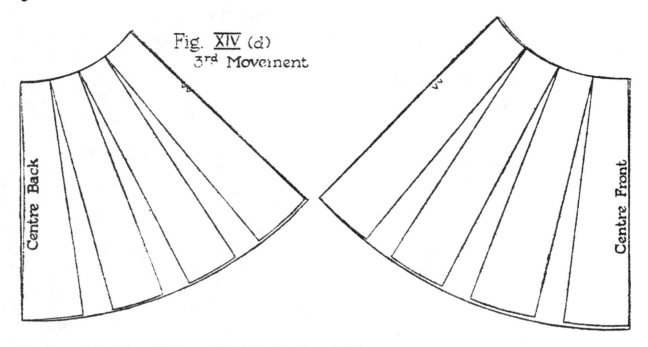

Fig. XIV (d)
3rd Movement

Centre Back

Centre Front

Dress 5. (Fig. XV.)   With Godet Skirt.

POINTS TO BE NOTED

The bodice is cut in one piece from shoulder to hip line, with the waist line defined by the belt.

The shoulder has a dart.

The front fastening edge is scalloped and is divided into 7 scallops. It overwraps about 1 in. beyond centre front.

The V of the neck is probably about 5 in. deep.

The skirt is made up of 8 godets of equal width, each rounded off at the top to form a scalloped hip line.

The godets are probably about twice as wide at the bottom edge as at the top.

MEASUREMENTS NECESSARY

Pin a tape round the natural hip line.

Shoulder to hip: 24 in.   Width of hip: 40 in.
Shoulder to hem: 45 in.

METHOD OF ADAPTATION

The pattern is worked in 2 movements:

1. Bodice adaptation and skirt foundation.
2. Godet.

1ST MOVEMENT. Fig. XV (a)

Rule centre front line 1 in. in from right-hand edge of paper (this allows for the overwrap).

Pin shoulder dart and place on the block pattern as before, except that the back and front should be put together so that they touch at the hip line.

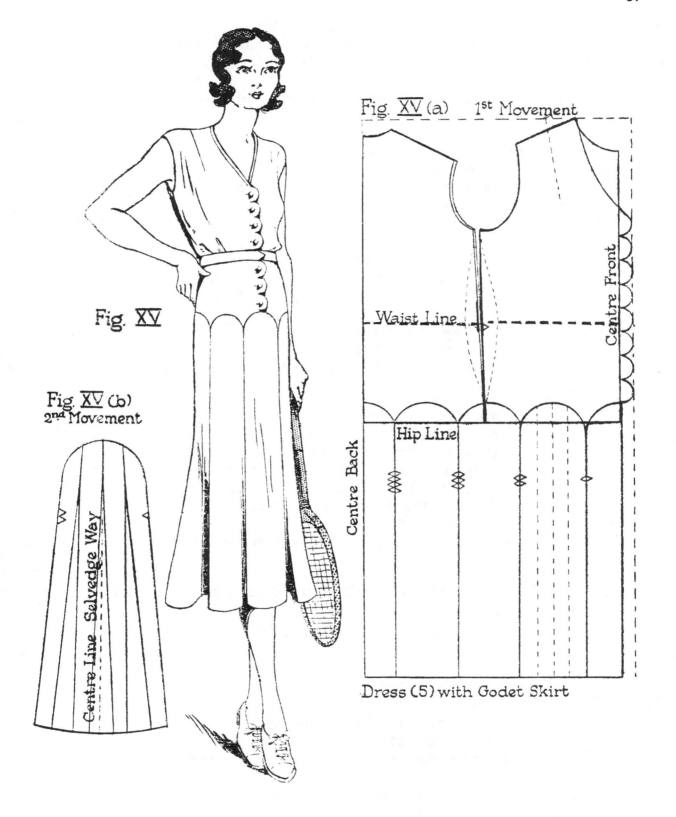

Fig. XV

Fig. XV (b)
2nd Movement

Centre Line   Selvedge Way

Fig. XV (a)   1st Movement

Centre Front

Waist Line

Centre Back

Hip Line

Dress (5) with Godet Skirt

This is more convenient for shaping the skirt.

The space between the centre front and centre back lines must be the exact half hip measure and must be tested before proceeding and altered if necessary.

Note : As the block pattern has presumably been drafted some time previously, it is not safe to trust to the hip measure being the same as that taken for this dress.

In a dress of this type any inaccuracy in the hip measure would cause a misfit which would be most difficult to rectify.

Outline block pattern and continue centre back and centre front lines to the hem line.

Divide the hip line into 4 equal sections, giving half a section at the front and back, as shown in the diagram.

The top of each section is curved, the highest part of the curve being $1\frac{1}{2}$ in. above the hip line. All the curves must be exactly alike.

Measure down from the neck in front 5 in., and draw in V, with a slight curve.

Divide the front edge, from the lowest point of V to the skirt line, into 7 equal sections and draw in scallops.

The under-arm seam may be shaped in slightly at the waist if desired.

2ND MOVEMENT. Fig. XV (b)

All the godets are the same and may be cut from the same pattern.

Cut away one part of the skirt and divide into four equal sections.

Cut along the divisions from the hem line to $\frac{1}{8}$ in. of top edge.

Rule a vertical line and place the part of the skirt on the paper so that the line runs down the centre. Spread out the sections, spacing them evenly so that the bottom edge is twice the width of the top.

Outline the godet and cut out.

In cutting the godets in material the centre should be straight with the selvedge.

Dress 6. (Fig. XVI.) Dress with Hip Yoke, Panels, and Circular Side Pieces.

This pattern shows a much more elaborate adaptation and illustrates the simplicity of obtaining an apparently difficult pattern from the block pattern.

POINTS TO BE NOTED

The bodice of this design fits the figure closely.

The skirt joins the bodice at the natural waist line.

The front and back panels of the skirt are cut in one piece with the pointed hip yoke.

The lowest point of the hip yoke is apparently at the natural hip line.

The side pieces are cut in a semi-circular flare.

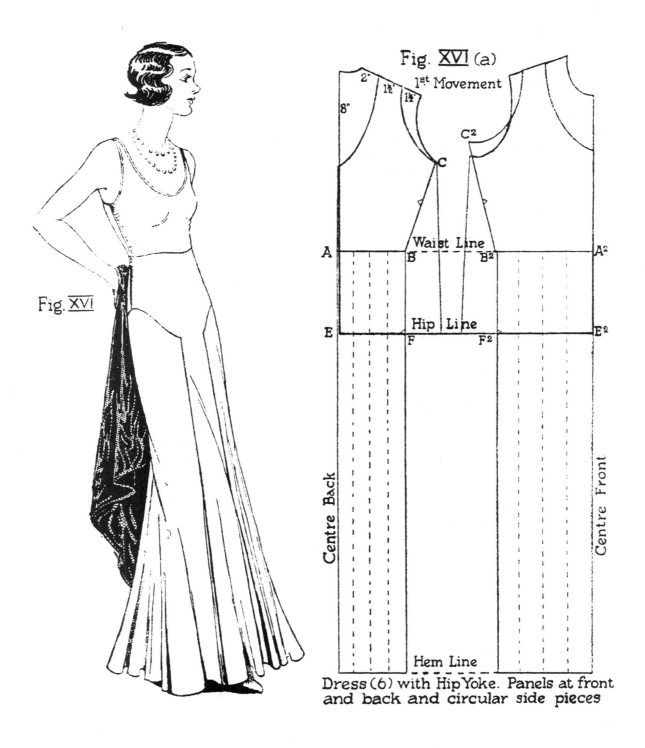

Fig. XVI

Fig. XVI (a)

1st Movement

2" 1½ 1½

8"

C²

C

A   B   Waist Line   B²   A²

E   F   Hip Line   F²   E²

Centre Back

Centre Front

Hem Line

Dress (6) with Hip Yoke. Panels at front
and back and circular side pieces

MEASUREMENTS NECESSARY

Pin tapes round the natural waist and hip lines.

Shoulder to waist:	17 in.	Width at waist:	28 in.
Shoulder to hip:	24 in.	Width at hip:	40 in.
Shoulder to hem:	54 in.		

METHOD OF ADAPTATION

The dress is worked out in 4 movements:

1. Adaptation of bodice and skirt foundation.
2. Skirt widened to fit at hip.
3. Hip yoke and panels—foundation of side godet.
4. Side godets.

1ST MOVEMENT. Fig. XVI (*a*)

Proceed as for Dress 4, Fig. XIV (*a*), without making any pleat or tucks on shoulder.

AB	$\frac{1}{4}$ waist, less 1 in.
A^2B^2	$\frac{1}{4}$ waist $+$ 1 in.
C	Under-arm point as on back of block pattern.
	Rule BC.
C^2	1 in. to $1\frac{1}{2}$ in. above the under-arm point of front of block pattern. Rule B^2C^2
	This raised point gives a closer fit round arm-hole.
	The front edge of the under-arm seam is gathered to the back edge.
	The arm-hole and neck may be shaped out if desired, as shown in diagram. but it is the wiser plan to leave this till the bodice is fitted.
	Rule vertical lines from B and B^2 to hem line.
EF	Hip line at back.
E^2F^2	Hip line in front.

2ND MOVEMENT. Fig. XVI (*b*)

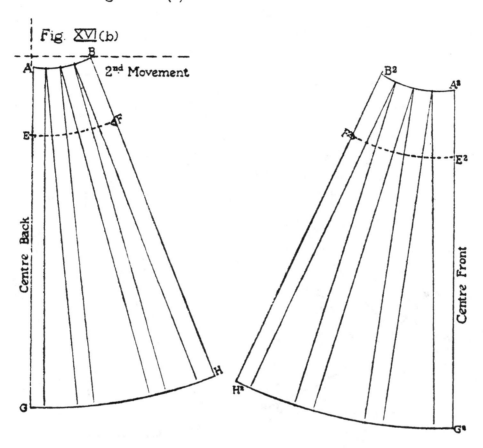

Proceed as for 2nd Movement in Dress 4, Fig. XIV (*b*).

EF	$\frac{1}{4}$ hip, less 1 in.
E^2F^2	$\frac{1}{4}$ hip + 1 in.
	Outline the pattern.
GH	Hem line at back.
G^2H^2	Hem line on front.

3RD MOVEMENT. Fig. XVI (*c*)

Place the two parts of the skirt together with *BH* and *B²H²* touching.

As the hip yoke has a point at the side it is necessary to have the seam exactly half-way between the centre front and centre back and not in a line with the under-arm seam as at present.

I	Half-way between *A* and *A²*.
J	Half-way between *G* and *G²*. Rule *IJ*.

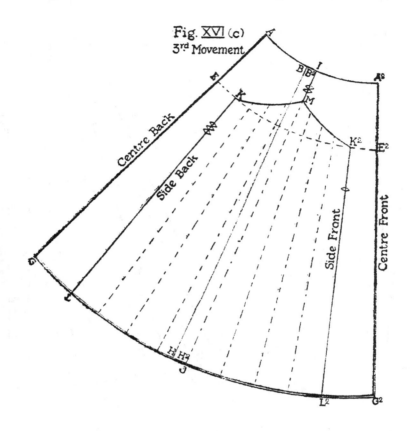

Fig. XVI (c)
3rd Movement.

The panel appears to be about 6 in. wide at the highest point and twice that width at the bottom.

EK	3 in. (½ width of panel at top.)
GL	6 in. Rule *KL*.
E²K²	3 in.
G²L²	6 in. Rule *K²L²*.
IM	(Seam of yoke), apparently about 4 in.
	Curve *K* to *M*, and *K²* to *M*.

Cut away the two panels, taking care to mark the centre front and back.

4TH MOVEMENT. Fig. XVI (*d*) and (*e*)

Divide the side piece of skirt into 8 equal sections. Cut along **the divisions** from the hem to $\frac{1}{8}$ in. of the yoke line. Two ways of cutting the flared side pieces are shown.

1. Forming a complete semicircle—thus giving a skirt hem of about 7 yd.

This is suitable for very soft thin material only.

2. Forming a quarter circle. The bottom edge in this case would be approximately 4yds.

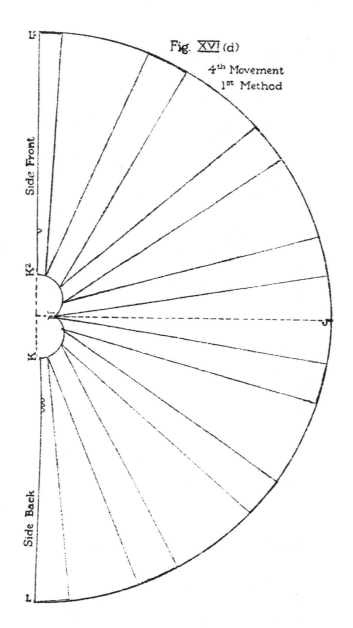

Fig. XVI (d)

4th Movement
1st Method

1ST METHOD. Fig. XVI (d)

Spread out the sections at an equal distance from each other as shown, so that *MJ* is horizontal and *KL* and *K²L²* are in a line with each other and at a right angle to *MJ*.

Outline the pattern at hem, thus drawing a complete semicircle. Outline hip line.

2ND METHOD. Fig. XVI (*e*)

Spread out the sections so that *K²L²* lies at a right angle to *KL* as in diagram.

MJ will bisect the right angle thus formed.

Outline the quarter circle of the hem.

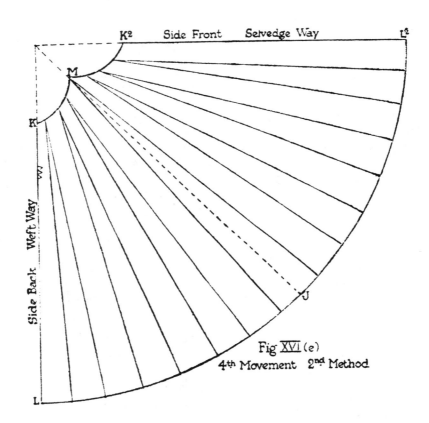

Fig XVI (*e*)
4th Movement 2nd Method

Note : It is not necessary to cut the completed patterns of these side pieces in paper.

The sections may be spread out equally well on the material but must be carefully placed and firmly pinned.

In 1st Method : *K²L²* and *KL* must be straight with the selvedge, and *MJ* straight with the weft.

In 2nd Method : *K²L²* lies straight with the selvedge : *KL* lies straight with the weft : *MJ* lies on direct cross of material.

Dress 7. (Fig. XVII.) **With Flounces.**

POINTS TO BE NOTED

The dress consists of 5 different parts:
1. Bodice, fitted in to natural waist line.
2. Hip yoke extending about 1 in. below natural hip line.
3. 1st flounce.
4. 2nd flounce. (The flounces appear to be equal in length.)
5. Foundation from which to hang 2nd flounce.

MEASUREMENTS NECESSARY

Pin tapes round the natural waist line and about 1 in. below natural hip line.

Shoulder to waist:	17 in.	Width at waist:	28 in.
Shoulder to hip:	25 in.	Width at hip:	42 in.
Shoulder to hem:	45 in.		

METHOD OF ADAPTATION

The pattern is worked out in 3 movements:
1. Bodice and skirt foundation.
2. Hip yoke and foundation of flounces.
3. Flounces.

1ST MOVEMENT. Fig. XVII (*a*)

As for Dress 4, Fig. XIV (*a*).

2ND MOVEMENT. Fig. XVII (*b*)

Proceed as for Dress 4, Fig. XIV (*b*).
Draw in AB and A^2B^2 the line of hip yoke at back and front.
Cut away the pattern of hip yoke.
The remainder of the skirt is divided into two equal lengths by lines CD and C^2D^2.
These lines indicate the lower edge of 1st flounce.
Trace off the pattern of this flounce ($ABCD$ and $A^2B^2C^2D^2$) on another piece of paper and cut out.
Draw lines EF and E^2F^2 1 in. above CD and C^2D^2. These lines mark the upper edge of 2nd flounce, thus allowing the two flounces to slightly overlap.
Cut along EF and E^2F^2.
Mark GH and G^2H^2 at hem line.
The skirt is now in 4 parts.
1. Hip yoke.
2. First flounce ($ABCD$ and $A^2B^2C^2D^2$).
3. Foundation from which to hang the second flounce ($ABEF$ and $A^2B^2E^2F^2$).
4. 2nd flounce $EFGH$ and $E^2F^2G^2H^2$.
Each part should be distinctly labelled and the centre back and front lines marked.

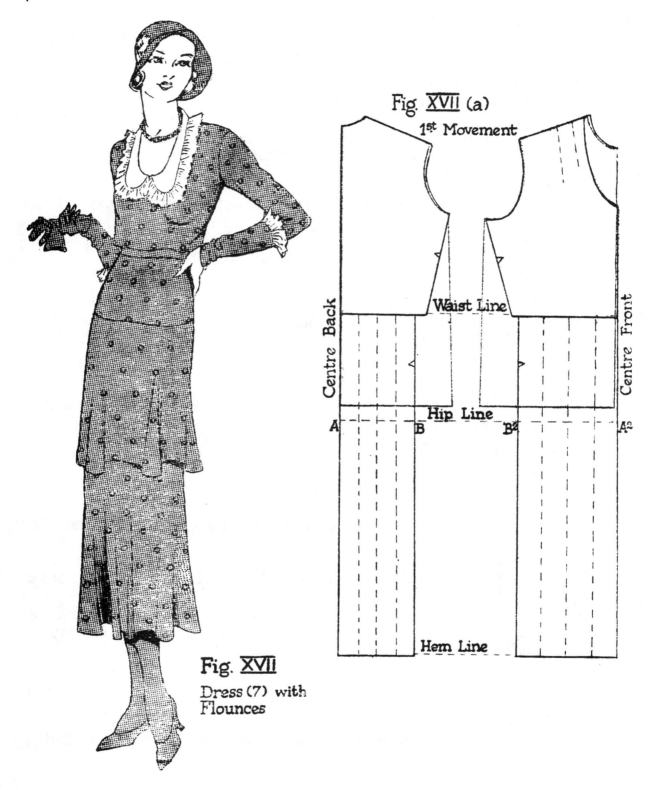

Fig. XVII (a)

1st Movement

Centre Back

Centre Front

Waist Line

Hip Line

A　　　　　B　　　　　B² 　　　　A²

Hem Line

Fig. XVII

Dress (7) with
Flounces

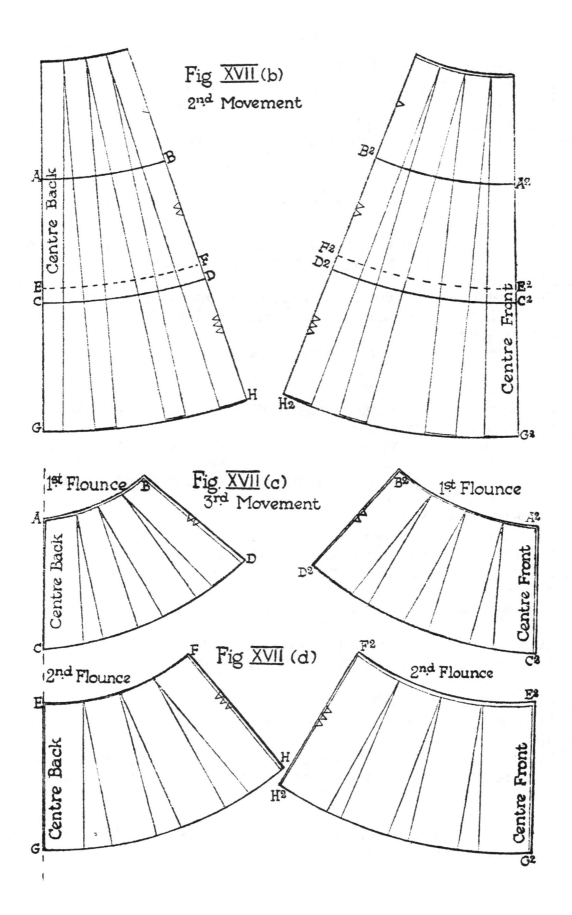

Fig XVII (b)
2nd Movement

Centre Back

A
B
E
F
D
C
G
H

B2
A2
F2
D2
E2
C2
H2
G2

Centre Front

Fig. XVII (c)
3rd Movement

1st Flounce

A
B
C
D

Centre Back

B2
D2
A2
C2

1st Flounce

Centre Front

Fig XVII (d)

2nd Flounce

F
E
H
G

Centre Back

F2
H2
E2
G2

2nd Flounce

Centre Front

3RD MOVEMENT. Fig. XVII(c) and (d)

Both flounces have to be flared out still further.

This is done in the usual manner, as shown in Fig. XVII (c) and (d)

The design does not appear to have a great deal of fulness at the bottom edge of the flounces, so a space of 1 in. only has been allowed between the sections, but this may be widened if desired.

Dress 8, with Flared Skirt Reduced in Width to 54 in.

POINTS TO BE NOTED

The dresses previously shown have all had the line of the skirt gradually widening from waist to hip and continuing in the same line, or in a still wider flare to the hem.

This sketch shows a skirt with a hip yoke which can be cut on similar lines to that of Dress 5, but the skirt, although flared at the hem, is probably not more than 54 in. wide.

The other points to be noted will be taken in the course of the adaptation.

MEASUREMENTS NECESSARY

Pin tapes round the natural waist and hip lines (the lower edge of the yoke appears to be at the natural hip line).

Shoulder to waist:	17 in.	Width at waist:	28 in.
Shoulder to hip:	24 in.	Width at hip:	40 in.
Shoulder to hem:	45 in.	Width at hem:	54 in.

METHOD OF ADAPTATION

The dress is worked out in 4 movements:
1. Bodice adaptation and skirt foundation.
2. Skirt widened to fit at hip.
3. Hip yoke and panel.
4. Lower part of skirt reduced to desired width.

1ST AND 2ND MOVEMENTS. Fig. XVIII (a). (2 not shown.)

Same as for Dress 6. (See Fig. XVI (a) and (b))

3RD MOVEMENT. Fig. XVIII (b)

Place the two parts of the skirt together as in Fig. XVI (c). Mark *AB* at hip line.

The front panel is cut in one piece with the upper part of the hip yoke, and is apparently about 2 in. wide at the highest point and 3 in. at the hem.

BC   2 in.

D   3 in. from centre front at hem line.

The upper line of the yoke appears to be 2 in. above the hip line.

Rule *DC* and continue 2 in. to *E*.

Dress 8.

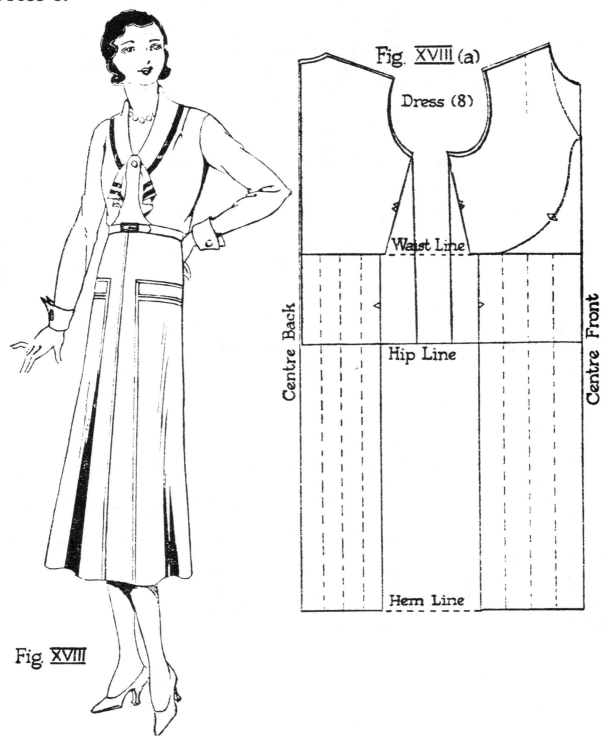

Fig. XVIII (a)

Dress (8)

Waist Line

Centre Back

Hip Line

Centre Front

Hem Line

Fig. XVIII

FE   (Upper line of yoke), parallel to *AC* and 2 in. above it.
            The side seam remains unaltered.
            Mark all the parts of the pattern very carefully to simplify cutting
              and putting together the material.
            Note that there is a seam at centre front and not a fold.
            Measure the width at hem and note (approximately 36 in.).

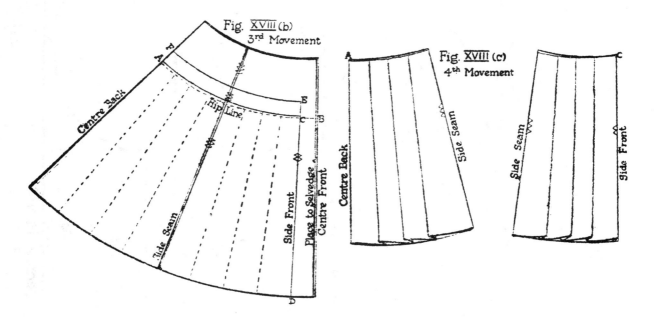

4TH MOVEMENT. Fig. XVIII (*c*)

    Cut away the front and back of the lower part of the skirt (not including the front panel).

    Divide each part into 4 equal sections, and cut from hem to $\frac{1}{8}$ in. of hip line.

    The skirt has to be reduced from 36 in. to 27 in. (half of 54 in., the desired width at hem).

    Each part has, therefore, to be reduced by $4\frac{1}{2}$ in.

    Place the back and front to the straight edge of the paper as for a flared skirt, but reverse the process and overlap the sections evenly so that the bottom edge is reduced to the desired amount.

CHAPTER VIII

SLEEVES

THE two sleeves shown are adapted from the blouse sleeve pattern.

MEASUREMENTS REQUIRED

Armhole:	16 in.
Width of sleeve:	15 in.
Outside length:	23 in.
Elbow width:	12 in.
Wrist:	8 in.

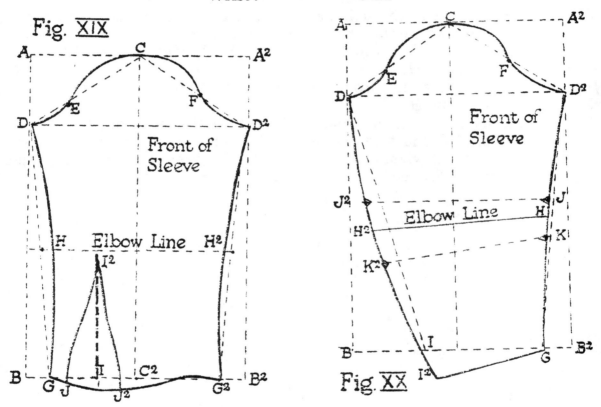

Fig. XIX

Front of Sleeve

Elbow Line

Fig. XX

Front of Sleeve

Elbow Line

Sleeve 1. (Fig. XIX.) Fitted Sleeve with Dart.

Draft as for blouse sleeve. (Fig. IV.)
Rule in guide line from H to H^2. (Elbow line.)

I Halfway between C^2 and G.
Rule guide line from I to elbow line.

I^2 1 in. below the elbow line on this guide line.

Measure G to G^2. Subtract from this amount the wrist measurement. This gives the amount to be taken in dart.

J and *J*²   Measured on either side of *I* half the amount to be taken out in the dart.

               Draw in the lines for the dart from *I*² to *J* and *J*², curving slightly inwards just below *I*² and then slightly outwards towards *J* and *J*².

Sleeve 2. (Fig. XX.)   Fitted Sleeve with Gathers at Elbow.

     The guiding lines and the head of the sleeve are drafted as for blouse sleeve. (Fig. IV.)

*B*²*G*   2 in. Rule guide line *D*²*G* and find centre.

H   ½ in. to left of centre point. Curve from *D*² through *H* to *G*.

GI   Wrist measure.

*I*²   1 in. below *I*. Rule *GI*². Rule *DI*² and find centre.

*H*²   Rule from *H* through the centre of *DI*² and extend to the amount of elbow measurement. Mark *H*² at end.

               Draw from *D* through *H*² to *I*². (Back edge of seam.)

J   1 in. above *H*.

*J*²   Measure distance from *D*² to *J*. Mark *J*² an equal distance from *D*.

K   1 in. below *H*.

*K*²   Measure *G* to *K* and mark *K*² an equal distance from *I*².

               *J*² and *K*² must be marked with notches on the pattern and on the material when cut. The material between *J*² and *K*² is gathered to set between *J* and *K* when the seam is joined.

CHAPTER IX

COLLARS AND CAPES

A COLLAR may be drafted, adapted from the block pattern or modelled on the figure.

The upright fitting collar of the tailor type is usually drafted.

Flat collars or capes which lie flat on the shoulder and neck of the garment, are usually modelled or adapted from the block pattern.

As the appearance of the garment may be made or marred by the collar, it is advisable to cut the entire collar in tissue paper and try it on the wearer before cutting the material.

Detachable Polo Collar.

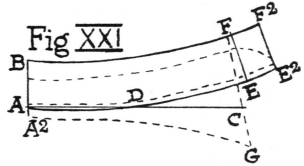

Neck Measurement 14 in.

The collar is in 3 parts, which are drafted simultaneously and must be traced off on separate pieces of paper afterwards.

    1. The collar band. (Solid black line.)
    2. The flap or turnover. (Dotted black line.)
    3. Neck band to be attached to blouse. (Dotted red line.)

1. COLLAR BAND

AB	$1\frac{1}{2}$ in. (Depth of collar at centre back.)
AC	$\frac{1}{2}$ neck measure (taken loosely round the base of the neck).
D	Centre of AC.
CE	1 in. to $1\frac{1}{2}$ in. Draw ADE (lower edge of band), keeping straight from A to D and curving upwards to E.
EF	Ruled at right angle to DE and same length as AB. Draw BF parallel to ADE.
E^2 and F^2	Continue DE and BF for 1 in. (or amount of overwrap at front of blouse). Rule F^2E^2. (Front edge of band.)

2. FLAP

> This meets in centre front, therefore no extra length for overwrap is required.

CG 1 in. Rule *FG*. (Front edge of flap. This may be sloped forward or farther back if desired.)

BF Top edge of flap—same as for collar band.

AA² ¼ in. Draw *A²* to *G*, keeping parallel to *AD*, then curving down to a point at *G*.

3. NECKBAND

This is cut on the same lines as the collar band, but is only 1 in. wide, and the front overwrap is sloped off at the top, as in Fig. XXI.

Rever Collar.

(As in design for Blouse 2. Fig. X. Also suitable for coat overall, Fig. XI.)

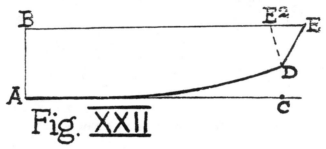

Neck Measurement 16 in.

This is the simplest possible collar. It is attached to the blouse at the normal neck line, therefore the neck measurement is taken from the actual garment and not the person. Measure carefully along the fitting line.

AB 2½ in. (Depth of collar at centre back—never more than 3 in.)

AC ½ neck measure. (The neck line.)

CD 1 in. Draw *AD*, keeping straight for about half the length, then curving upwards to *D*.

BE At right angle to *AB* and 1 in. longer than *AC*.
  Rule *DE*. This gives the slight point in front as seen in the collar of Blouse 2, Fig. X.

If a straight end is desired, rule as shown by *DE²* at a right angle to the neck line.

The collar is cut selvedge way in double material, with a folded edge at the outside edge of collar (*BE²*).

Roll Collar, with Points.

The measurement of the neck is taken on the wearer, measuring round the neck to the lowest part of the V in front according to the desire of the wearer.

Fig. XXIII

Neck Measurement 22 in.

AB	3 in. (Depth of collar at centre back.)
AC	½ neck measurement.
CD	¾ in. Draw *AD*, keeping straight about ⅓ of way.
BE	At right angle to *AB*, and 1½ in. longer than *AC*, to allow for point in front.
	Rule *DE*.

Collars and Capes Adapted from Block Pattern.

A collar or a cape which lies flat on the shoulders and at the neck line may be adapted from the block pattern.

It is not advisable to cut the collar pattern until the dress has been fitted and the desired neck line marked.

The block pattern may then have the corrected neck line drawn in, and if any alteration has been made in the shoulder seam this also should be corrected in the block pattern.

In all the collars and capes of this type which are shown here (with the exception of Fig. XXVIII), the same procedure is followed in placing the block pattern on the paper preparatory to the adaptation.

Place the centre back straight with the edge of the paper.

Place the front of the pattern so that the shoulder seam touches that of the back and with the neck lines meeting.

Trace in the line of the neck (corrected line), and draw the collar pattern in one piece according to the design being followed.

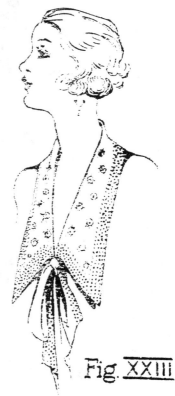

Fig. XXIII

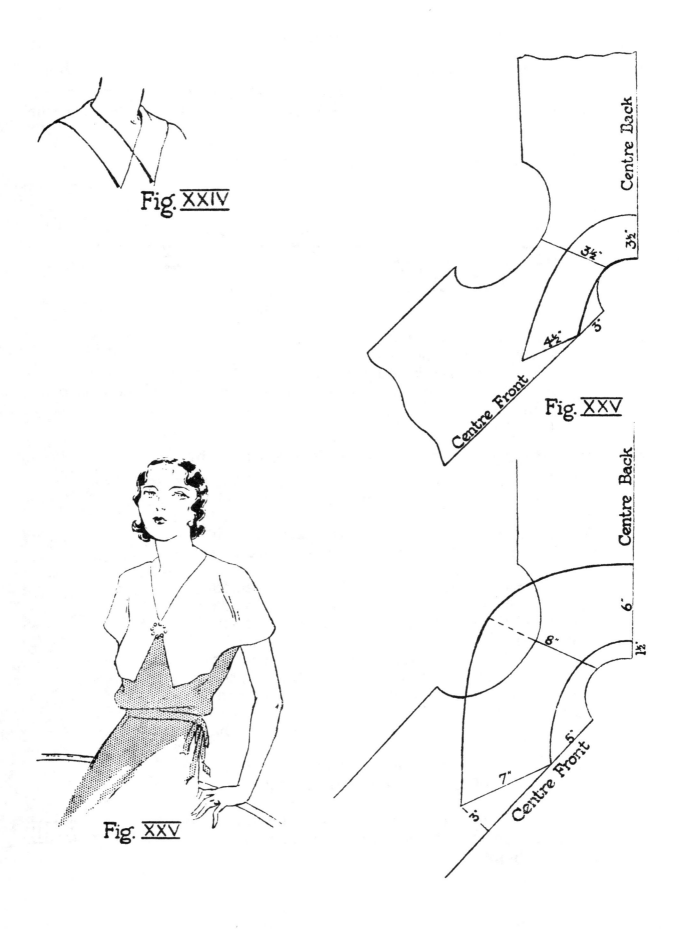

Fig. XXIV

Fig. XXV

Fig. XXV

Centre Back

Centre Front

3½"

3¼"

4½"

3"

Centre Back

6"

8"

1½"

7"

5"

3"

Centre Front

Fig. XXIV and Fig. XXV show simple round collars with points in front. Measurements are given in the diagram but only as a guide.

The cutter will find it much better to trust to her own sense of line for width and for sloping the points, etc.

In the other patterns measurements are not given.

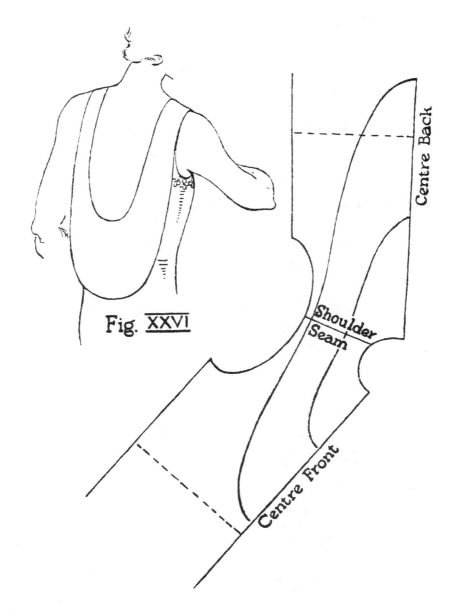

Fig. XXVI

Fig. XXVI is a flat cape collar for a rather elaborate evening dress, and is suitable for heavy lace or for a beaded design.

The front and back are cut to a fold of the material, and there is a seam on the shoulder.

Fig. XXVII has a similar cape effect, but is suitable for softer material.

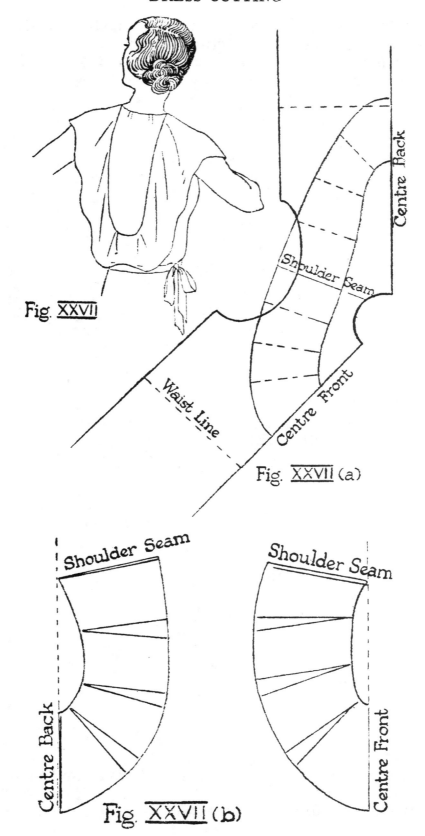

Fig. XXVII

Fig. XXVII (a)

Fig. XXVII (b)

The flat shape is taken as for Fig. XXVI and then slashed at intervals so that it can be opened out to give the full fluted edge.

Fig. XXVIII has a closer fit round the outside edge than the others.

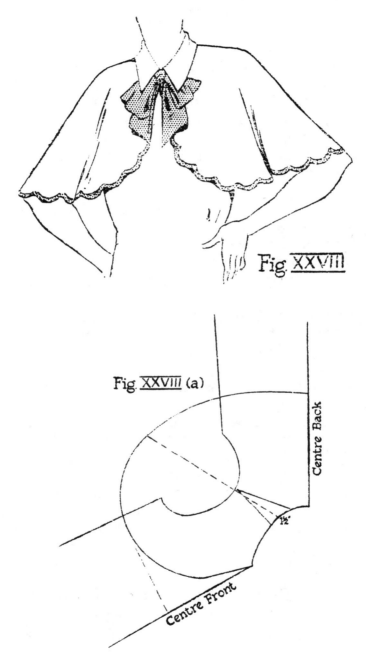

Fig. XXVIII

Fig. XXVIII (a)

Instead of placing the shoulder seams of back and front of block pattern together let them meet at the armhole, but leave a space of $1\frac{1}{2}$ in. at the neck points. This forms a dart on the shoulder, and the outside edge of the cape will then fit more closely round the arms.

CHAPTER X

PLEATED SKIRTS

I⊤ is not always realized that unless a skirt is set on to a deep-fitted hip yoke it is extremely difficult to make a pleated skirt from a straight length of material.

Many skirts have straight panels of pleats let in, possibly at the back and front. The remainder of the skirt is cut from a simple gored pattern. It is not proposed to deal with such skirts here.

It will be found that most of the pleated skirts of the present day have the pleats slightly sloping outwards towards the hem. This ensures a good set to the pleats.

As has been said elsewhere, the bottom edge of a pleated skirt should measure 45 in. to 54 in. in width, exclusive of pleats.

The amount of material allowed for pleats varies according to the thickness of the material and the spacing of the pleats.

Pleats on heavy thick material are seldom less than 2 in. deep, and frequently they are $2\frac{1}{2}$ in.

Thin material may have pleats of any width desired.

For each pleat twice its finished width must be allowed.

When joins have to be made in the skirt it should be arranged that the seams come under a pleat, but not on the fold.

Pleats should be as nearly as possible on the straight of the material if they are to set in place.

The method shown here of working up the pleats in tissue paper over the lines of the foundation pattern is satisfactory and very exact.

It is absolutely imperative that the lines of all pleats be clearly marked in thread-marking on the material so that the pleats may be set correctly.

As pleats are bulky, care must be taken to obtain an easy but good fit at the hip line.

None of the dresses shown in Chapter VII have pleated skirts, but the method of working the pleats out in tissue paper, as shown in this chapter, may be used equally well on a dress pattern.

Skirt 5. (Fig. XXIX.) Pleated Skirt on Hip Yoke.

This skirt is worked on a foundation similar to Skirt 4, Fig. VIII. The width at hem, exclusive of pleats, is 54 in., but may, if desired, be rather less (45 in. or 50 in.).

1ST MOVEMENT

As for Skirt 2, Fig. VI.

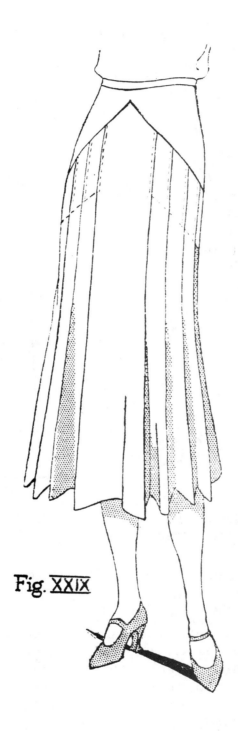

Fig. XXIX

2ND MOVEMENT

Proceed as for Skirt 2.

Draw in the line of the hip yoke. (Fig. XXIX (*a*).) In the **design** the yoke

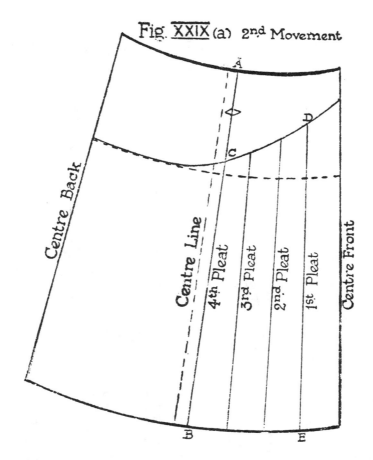

Fig. XXIX (a) 2nd Movement

line appears to follow the hip line at the back almost as far as the side seam, from which point it curves upwards to a point in the centre front about $1\frac{1}{2}$ in. below the waist.

AB   Side seam. 1 in. in front of the centre line of skirt as in Skirt 2, Fig. VI (*b*).

C   Where *AB* crosses the yoke line.

The lines of the pleats must be ruled off on the foundation pattern. In the design the pleats slope slightly outward from the centre front, forming a front panel with 4 pleats on each side of it. The panel is apparently about 5 in. wide at the top and 7 in. at the bottom edge.

D   Measure in from the centre front line to touch the yoke line $2\frac{1}{2}$ in. (half width of panel at top).

E $3\frac{1}{2}$ in. from centre front on the hem line ($\frac{1}{2}$ width of panel at bottom edge).

Rule *DE*, the line of the 1st pleat.

There are altogether 4 pleats on each side of the front. Divide the space between *DE* and *CB* into 3 equal parts, and rule lines to mark the remaining 3 pleats.

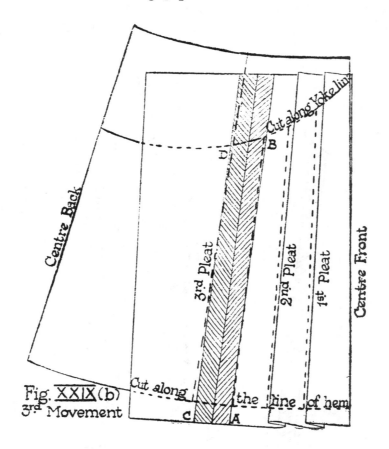

Fig. XXIX (b)
3rd Movement

3RD MOVEMENT. Fig. XXIX (b)

Two or more sheets of tissue paper joined together will be necessary for this part of the pattern.

The pattern has pleats $1\frac{1}{2}$ in. wide when finished, therefore 3 in. is allowed for each pleat.

Pin the straight edge of the tissue paper to the centre front of the foundation pattern, taking care that there is sufficient length of tissue paper to cover the lower part of the foundation.

Trace the line of the 1st pleat as it shows through the tissue paper.

From this line measure to the left 3 in. (amount allowed for each pleat), and rule a parallel line.

Fold the tissue paper so that the 1st line touches the 2nd, thus forming a pleat $1\frac{1}{2}$ in. wide.

Pin through to the foundation.

Trace the line of the 2nd pleat and rule a parallel line 3 in. to left of it.

Pin the 2nd pleat. Proceed in a similar manner for the 3rd and 4th pleats.

Fig. XXIX(*b*) shows the 1st and 2nd pleats already formed, and the 3rd pleat ruled off preparatory to being folded over. *AB* will be folded over to meet *CD*.

When all the pleats are made, and before removing the pins, trace the lines of the yoke and hem as they show through the pleated tissue paper.

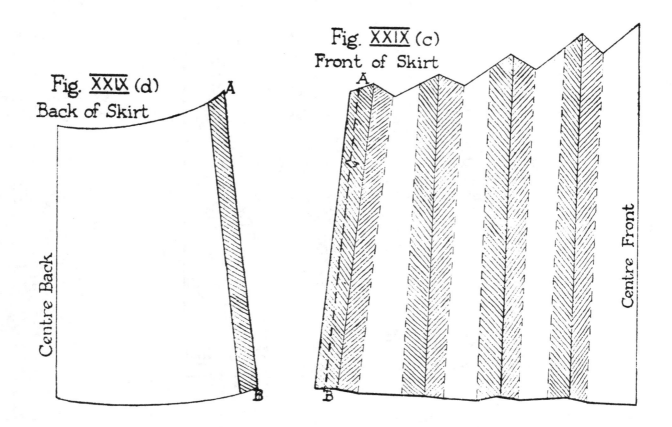

Fig. XXIX (*c*)
Front of Skirt

Fig. XXIX (*d*)
Back of Skirt

Cut the pleated paper along the lines of yoke and hem and down the side seam (the second line of the 4th pleat).

Open out the pattern and it will be found to be similar to Fig. XXIX (*c*).

Fig. XXIX (*d*) shows the back of the skirt unaltered.

4TH MOVEMENT. Fig. XXIX (*e*)

Cut away the yoke from the foundation pattern.

The waist line must be reduced to the ½ waist measure.

Proceed as for Skirt 4, Fig. VIII (*b*).

Make sure that the seam of the yoke runs in a line with the edge of the 4th pleat of the skirt.

The pattern is now in 4 parts:

1. Pleated front (in tissue paper).
2. Back of skirt.

3. Yoke front.
4. Yoke back.
It is better to avoid having a seam at the edge of the 4th pleat where the back joins the front.

By cutting away 1 in. from the side of the front, as shown by the dotted line AB, Fig. XXIX (c), and adding the part cut away to the back, as shown by red line AB, Fig. XXIX (d), the seam will be hidden under the pleat.

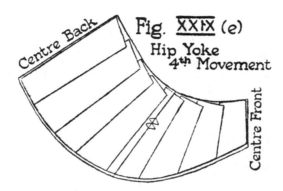

Fig. XXIX (e)
Hip Yoke
4th Movement

Skirt 6. Four Gored Skirt with Inverted Pleats at End of Seams.

This skirt is divided into 4 equal parts, or gores. Extra width is given at the hem by inverted pleats at each seam, extending from a few inches above the knee to the hem.

1ST MOVEMENT

As for Skirt 2, Fig. VI.

2ND MOVEMENT. Fig. XXX (a)

Proceed as for Skirt 2, but do not draw in the side seams.

The entire skirt consists of a back and front gore and two side gores of equal width.

Fig. XXX (a) shows the half pattern, i.e. half the front and back gores and the side gore.

AA^2 Waist line.
BB^2 Hem line.
CC^2 Hip line.
A^2D and $AE = \frac{1}{4} AA^2$.
B^2D^2 and $BE^2 = \frac{1}{4} BB^2$.

Rule EE^2 and DD^2 (seams of skirt).

The waist line must be reduced to the required width by darts at the seams.

Measure AA^2, and from the amount obtained subtract the $\frac{1}{2}$ waist measure.

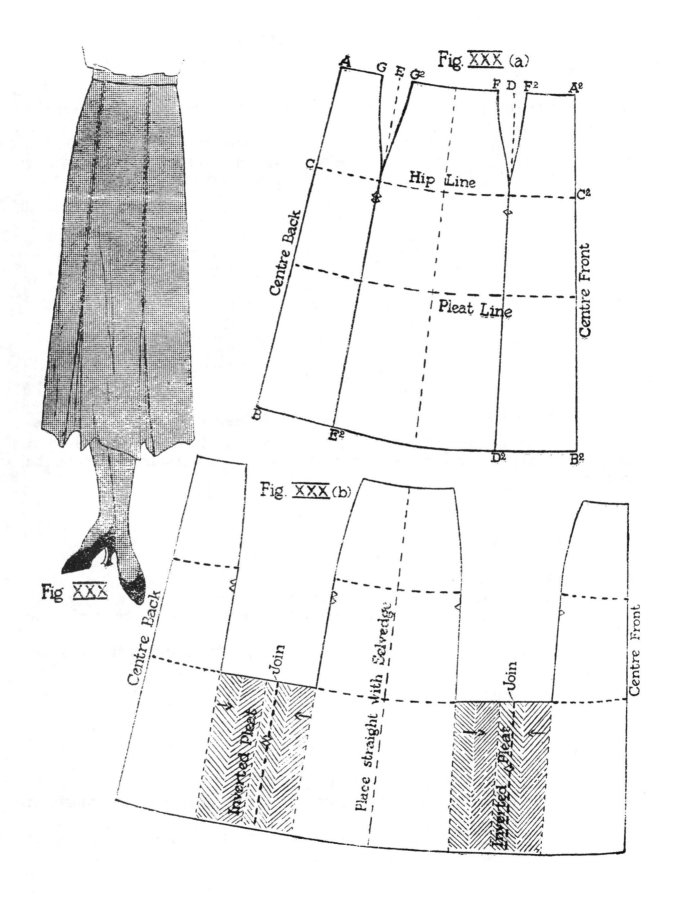

Fig. $\overline{XXX}$ (a)

A   G   E   G²   F D F²   A²

Centre Back

Centre Front

C   Hip Line   C²

Pleat Line

F²   D²   B²

Fig. $\overline{XXX}$ (b)

Centre Back

Join

Place straight with Selvedge

Join

Centre Front

Inverted Pleat

Inverted Pleat

Fig $\overline{XXX}$

This gives the amount of surplus material to be taken out in **darts** and is divided equally.

$$\left.\begin{array}{l} EG \\ EG^2 \\ DF \\ DF^2 \end{array}\right\} = \tfrac{1}{4} \text{ amount to be taken out in darts.}$$

Curve darts as for Skirt 2.

Note : It may be better to make smaller darts at the seams and an extra dart at the centre of the side gore.

3RD MOVEMENT. Fig. XXX (*b*)

In the skirt shown, there is an inverted pleat at the end of each seam, the pleats commencing 18 in. below the waist. The finished pleat is 2 in. ; therefore, as there is a pleat on each side of the seam, 8 in. extra width is required.

Cut out the parts of the skirt and spread them apart so that there is a space of 8 in. between each at the lower part of skirt.

It is unnecessary to cut the entire skirt again, as the extra width of paper for the pleats may be pinned to the end of the seams.

Rule the centre line to show where the inverted pleats meet.

Note the red dotted line, the suggested position for the join, thus avoiding a seam at the edge of a fold or where it will be easily seen.

This pattern may be used equally well with godets instead of inverted pleats at end of seams. (See Godets, Chapter XI, Fig. XXXI (*b*).)

In cutting out in material place the centre line of side gore as well as the centre front and back lines straight with the selvedge.

CHAPTER XI

GODETS

A GODET is a piece of material shaped like a section of a circle and let into a skirt to give extra width at the hem.

Fig. XXXI (*b*): a narrow godet suitable for skirts of thick material. Width at bottom edge 9 in. This is inserted into a straight slit in the skirt or at a seam.

Decide on the length of the slit *AB*. (Fig. XXXI (*a*).)

A^2B^2 (Central line of godet) = length of slit *AB*

C and *D*   Measured on either side of *B* the ½ width of godet.

         Rule A^2C and A^2D, sides of godet.

         Cut away the extra length at sides of godet to make them equal to *AB*.

         Curve bottom edge.

Fig. XXXI(*c*): This godet is cut from a quarter circle of material, and is suitable for skirts of thin material, such as georgette, etc.

A^2B^2 = length of slit *AB*.

A^2C = length of slit *AB* and at right angles to A^2B^2.

A^2D = length of slit and bisecting the angle at *A*.

         Curve B^2DC.

         A^2B^2 and A^2C are cut straight with the selvedge and weft of the material, thus bringing the centre of the godet on the true cross.

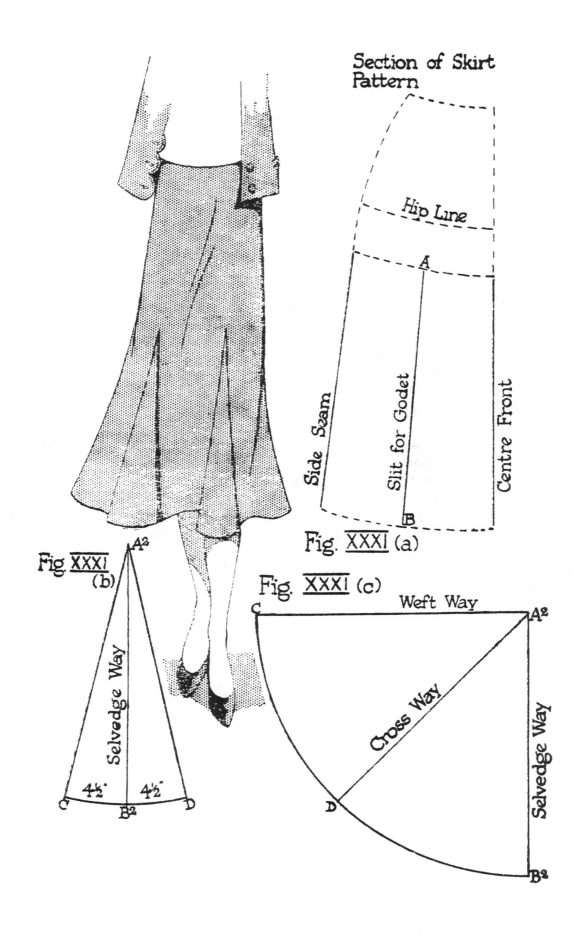

Section of Skirt Pattern

Hip Line

A

Side Seam

Slit for Godet

Centre Front

B

Fig. XXXI (a)

Fig. XXXI (b)

A²

Selvedge Way

4½"   4½"

C   B²

Fig. XXXI (c)

C   Weft Way   A²

Cross Way

Selvedge Way

D

B²

Fig. XXXII shows a godet of a different type. A shaped section is actually cut away from the skirt pattern and a godet inserted.

The pattern for the godet is obtained by flaring the cut-out section to the required width (in this case 12 in.).

A two-piece skirt may be used for the foundation pattern. (Skirt 2, Fig. VI (b).

Fig. XXXII (a) shows the front of the skirt pattern with the godets marked off.

Fig. XXXII (b) shows the half-front godet cut away from the pattern and divided into 2 equal parts.

Place so that centre front is straight and the other edge is spread out to the half-width of godet at bottom edge.

Fig. XXXII (c) shows the side godet divided into 4 equal parts. Place so that the centre of godet is straight and the sections are spaced out equally on each side of the centre to the width of the godet at bottom edge.

If desired, the godet may be kept straight for a few inches at the top and flared out below that.

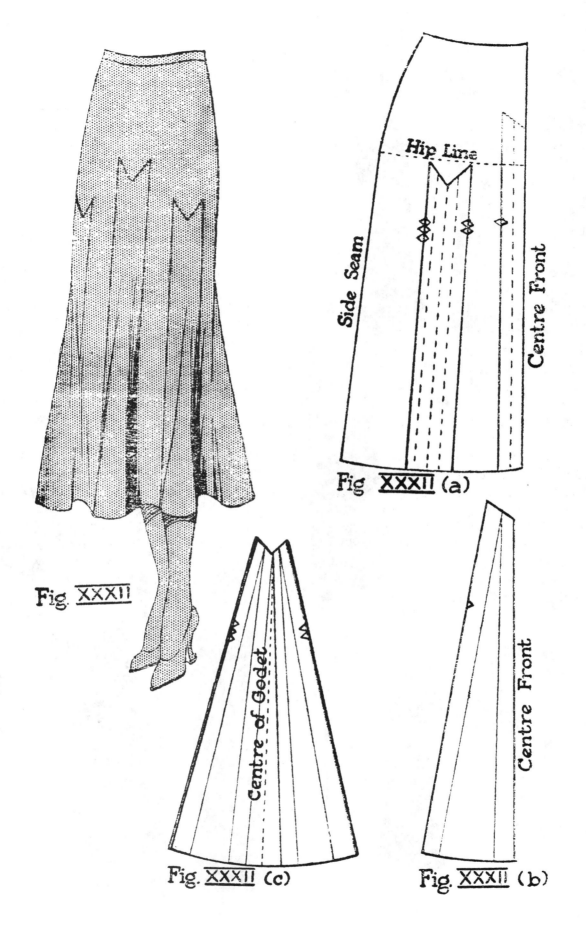

Fig. XXXII

Fig. XXXII (a)

Side Seam

Hip Line

Centre Front

Fig. XXXII (c)

Centre of Godet

Fig. XXXII (b)

Centre Front

72